Autism
Love
And
Neurosis

Jacqueline Freeston

Illustrated by Gertie Grace & Purple.
Graphic design Bethany Maria Downs

Kingdom Publishers

Autism Love and Neurosis

Copyright© Jacqueline Freeston

All rights reserved. No part of this book may be reproduced in any form by photocopying or any electronic or mechanical means, including information storage or retrieval systems, without permission in writing from both the copyright owner and the publisher of the book. The right of Jacqueline Freeston to be identified as the author of this work has been asserted by her in accordance with the Copyright, Designs and Patents Act 1988 and any subsequent amendments thereto. A catalogue record for this book is available from the British Library.

All Scripture Quotations have been taken from the New Living Translations.

ISBN: 978-1-911697-08-4

1st Edition by Kingdom Publishers

Kingdom Publishers

London, UK.

You can purchase copies of this book from any leading bookstore or email
contact@kingdompublishers.co.uk

New Living Translation

Dedication

To all those who know the Dark Night of the Soul.

Foreword

What I did by asking John Pantry to write the forward for this book, was to create a link between my first experience of becoming a Christian and this moment now. When I first became a Christian as a young adult, making it my choice over the weekly visits as a child to our local church. I had been invited to a Christian revival music concert in Margate, with Eric Delve speaking and John Pantry Playing. I felt such an immense power in the words I heard that evening and a real sense of the Holy Spirit washing over me as I listened to John's worship music. Without any control over me, my feet were propelled to the front of the marquee, and a weight came upon me, and I was kneeling to pray; I can still remember the sweet damp smell of soil and freshly cut grass...here I was committing my life to God. There were prayers and tears and later I bought Johns Album and waited in the queue for him to sign it. I am truly humbled and encouraged by Johns words and extremely blessed to be able to share these with you.

Jacqueline Freeston is a remarkable woman with a gift for storytelling and a vivid and rich life to write about. The death of her son Alan is the tragic focal point of a life lived for others and there have been numerous others to whom she has given a place of safety and security and on whom she has lavished her love. A Godly influence on all who have come her way, Jacqueline's faith and passion for life have sustained her in countless times of pain. However, you'll discover many joyful and humorous stories here too. This is a beautifully observed book about a life that will both challenge and move you. It certainly left me wanting to know more and asking - so what's next Jacqueline? I highly recommend it.

John Pantry

Content

Introduction	15
Patience	23
Red	30
Sorello	36
Parley	44
Ivy	50
Belle	56
Tsuin	64
Ana	72
Nabob	78
Mara	84
Ruth	90
Jejune	94
Solo And Emi	100
Little Pete	104
Ash	110
The Rabbit Hole	113
The Wavern	131
The Requiem	145
Emma	148
Emma's Story (Told By Emma)	159
Jules	170
The Goodness	177
Curly	195
My American Brother	201
Eliza	211
Turophile	217
Annika	227
Stefanie	233
Trio	239
Fortem	245
The Beginning	249

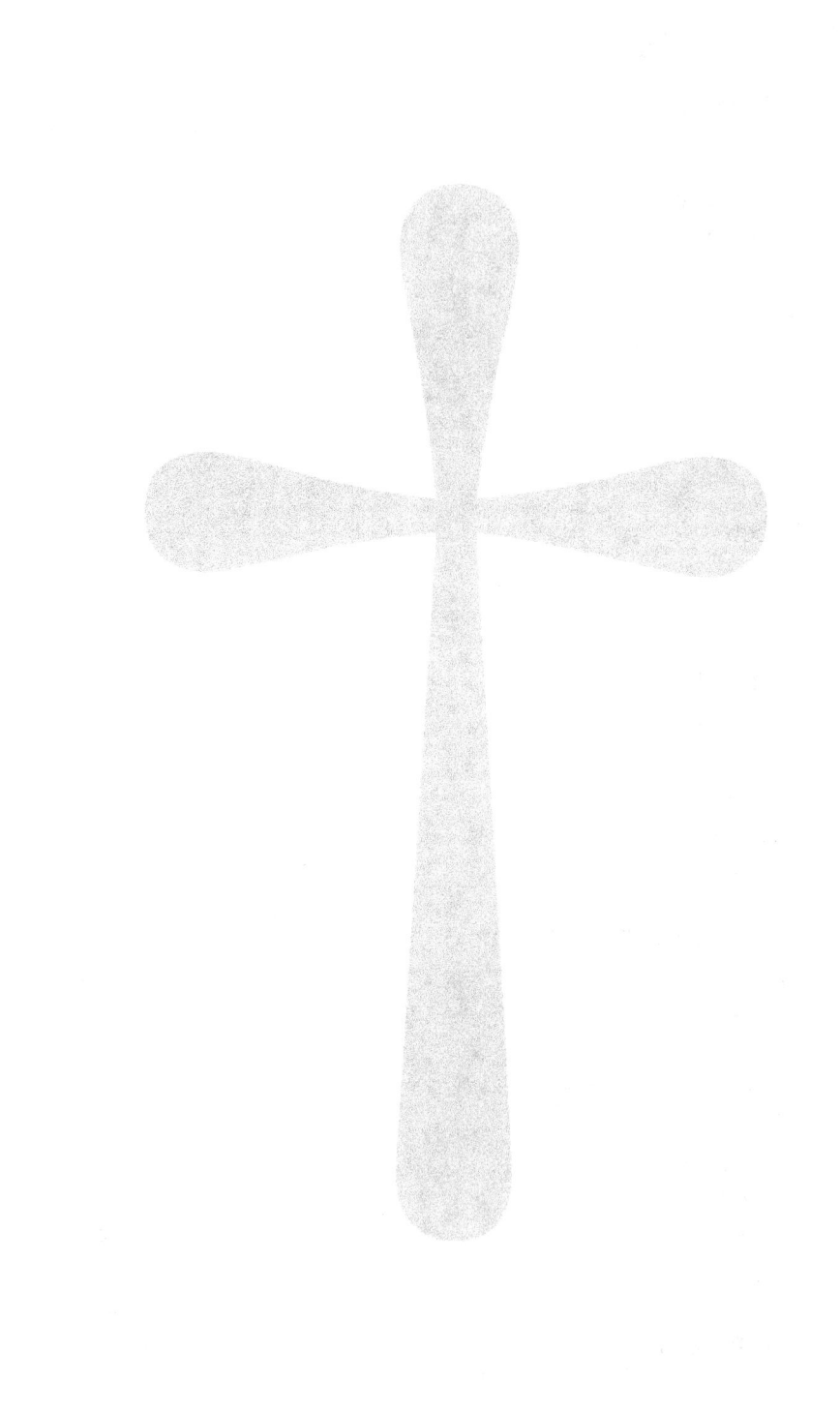

AUTISM LOVE AND NEUROSIS
A.L.A.N

†

INTRODUCTION

I have struggled to write this introduction, a whole life has already happened when God, unbeknown to me was shaping my path to get me to where I am today.

Jeremiah 29:11
For I know the plans I have for you," says the LORD. "They are plans for good and not for disaster, to give you a future and a hope. In those days when you pray, I will listen. If you look for me wholeheartedly, you will find me.

I Love this verse and use it a lot, mainly because it is one of those I can recall, when I find retaining information a challenge at times. Yet when reading this verse, I am reminded by Ministers that it does not stop there, we need to read the words and immerse ourselves into them. 'Look for me wholeheartedly'. These words are the instruction manual to access this support from God, we must seek him with all our heart in all that we do and we must remember that God knows our heart and so he knows if we are seeking him with all that we have. I will not lie, I find this the hardest, I get distracted, we all do. Temptation to everyday life is appealing, drinking with mates, eating out, a party or two, a little risk here and there. A shopping trip, binge TV watching, social media, the next drama at work. If we commit to God, we can have the most wonderful treasures in heaven and on earth as he provides for our needs. When we seek God, we do not just look for him with our eyes, although there is plenty of beautiful moments within nature to find the

Lord, we need to seek, so this means to read his word, spend time learning and sharing discussions in bible classes. Seek the lord through praise and worship and in the work that we do when we serve others.

With Jeremiah in mind, I knew I had to trust in God with this book, all that matters is the here and now, to introduce the story as the moment happened. You do not need all the boring history, the whys, and wherefores, just that I had moved my family every year for nine years. Now here I was, standing in front of a grade two listed building council property which needed some work and was registered on the exchange book, demanding God to make it happen. It felt that this was a risky thing I was doing then I remembered.

Joshua 1:9

This is my command—be strong and courageous! Do not be afraid or discouraged. For the LORD your God is with you wherever you go."

At the time, my relationship with God was vastly different to the one I have now. Yes, I prayed and praised and asked and gave but with hindsight I can see that my prayers were one sided. My giving was because it was the right thing to do and my asking was an expectation, so I added to my prayer a demand not unlike a bargain; similar to Hannah in 1 Samuel, she went right to the top in her desperate plea to have a son, promising if God gave her a son she would give him right back to God. I have never prayed such a prayer since that time, it felt completely irrational, yet the prayer I prayed was just that.

'Please father God if it is Your will, let us move in. This house has many rooms, and I will use them all for You. If You send someone, I will help them, it will be Your house not mine. I promise to make this house, work for You Lord. If you can just make it happen... come on Lord, make it happen! In Jesus precious name Amen.'

I gave the matter no other thought; I needed to be in this house nearer to my mum as she had been diagnosed with breast cancer. Treatment would be starting soon and the treatment, before anything else, was a mastectomy. I also had my middle son Jonathon under Great Ormond Street and not enough time for anything more. Then the exchange happened, like a smooth run of Jenga, all the pieces in the right place, snug and in order. This gave a true sense of the Lord at work, 'His will not mine'. No sooner had we moved in, than God acted on my prayer and sent this slight brown-haired mousey child to my door. I must add that all those who ended up at my door, to be invited in to stay a season or more are included in this short book and will be nicknamed appropriately to suit God's lesson or the personality of that person. There are of course name and event changes as many of those who came to our door are not contactable and the timeline is curved as time tends to be like that. There is a sense that only two years have passed when in fact it is twenty-one.

Why this book now? The relevance will come later but please know this is simply a written account of the room God has used throughout our time of living here.

Ecclesiastes 3

"For everything there is a season, a time for every activity under heaven."

What I need you to know as you read is that God, Yahweh, our Father is always working in our lives whether we see it or not. When you see it, you really must share your story as there is power in God's work and in the telling of the great things He has done.

ALL IN GOD'S TIMING....

THROUGH THE PINK DOOR

1
PATIENCE

Patience turned up one evening after my children got home from a Sea Cadet meeting. Sea Cadets was a definite form of respite for me, as life was crazy stupid at home with our youngest Jonathon and the seemingly endless journeys back and forth to Great Ormond Street. Patience looked like a young Sandra Bullock and hid behind my daughter's back on her first visit here. Twelve years old, chestnut brown hair and as quiet as a mouse, until I asked her in to eat and then food loosened her tongue and she told me about her abusive past. Patience was a 'looked after' child and clearly needed more looking after than she was getting. The care system had taken her from her drug addicted birth family to an abusive adopted family. From there she journeyed as many do, from foster home to foster home; finally, to residential settings, which provided some form of continuity amongst the trauma which (for her) had become a part of the norm. This girl was smart and used this opportunity placed before her of an established family home, she followed up the first visit with a second the very next day and a third shortly after that. It was not long before Patience felt settled enough with us that she refused to go home to her carers. The social worker was called, as were the foster carers. My hubby and I had no professionals to call so we ordered take out and had a family meeting. My eldest, Alan, was far too busy with computer tech to be bothered and agreed for Patience to stay if 'she' was not in his way. Cherrie, my daughter, felt it was a good idea and a nice thing to do. So, there it was, opportunity had opened a door - well that is how it was seen. However, it is as clear as when Jesus lifts the veil from our eyes, that Patience was the first of

God's children who needed a room and whether a person is in our lives for a moment or a season or longer, there is always a reason for it.

Of course - you saw it coming, the storm. It was brewing within the first few weeks and then six months in, it hit. The ceiling turned blue with the colourful language, and the house rocked as the anger from this mousey 12-year-old took hold. I was exhausted, the children were exhausted and Patience was burnt out with so much unregulated emotion. It is a dark cloud that forms when we feel so lost and question the destruction of our good intentions. I hated it, I wanted to help, to support and to guide. Patience however had other ideas. I was unaware at-this-time that Patience was reacting to Trauma, and we had been full on and were experiencing compassion fatigue. It was at this point that social services decided in their wisdom to remove her, the logic being that the family functioned perfectly well before she had arrived. There was no support, there was no notice, there was no time to prepare, and there was no goodbye - just the harsh coldness of the removal of a whole small human being from a place where they felt safe enough to explode. Patience was my first introduction to trauma and attachment disorder, the horrors of the scares that play out until they can be professionally addressed. Sadly, she was not going to address any of her issues soon. The harshness of the removal only served to bring her back the next day. Subconsciously I felt she knew she needed to keep this door open; she had been placed locally and so the visits continued. I had all the pleasure of raising her and watching her grow without the funding. I tried badly to work from our heavenly Father's perspective: don't worry, I know the plans I have for you. But it is not easy to have such a depth of faith when everything swamps you and it feels as if God is nowhere to be seen. Of course, this is when the Lord is often working at His best, but with human nature we fail to see it. Our faith becomes displaced and smoking and scratch cards seemingly become more reliable than God, who tells me He is in control.

We ended up with a further 208 weeks of regular visits from Patience, until she was finally old enough to leave the care system and despite advice from me, she left the little rental rooms to move into a house share.

It was not a legitimate house share and had all the markers of a sublet. I was so concerned and stressed my concerns each time Patience paid a bill.

'Be careful, do not register for council tax,' I told her.

After three months she had a council tax bill for £1200. She marched around my kitchen spitting feathers, outraged she had been billed for other people's arrears, shouting out loud, "It's not my bill to pay," I was trying to balance the phone on my ear, while endeavoring to keep her calm. Alan was eating his dinner and shouting back; 'If you had listened to my mother it would not have happened.' that sentence was not a direct quote, Alan's language was as equally as colourful as Patience's.

Patience was oblivious to his comments but not for long. As if the clocks had stopped, the fork that had been in my son's hand had sped into the air, just as Patience was screaming again the blue words 'It's not my bill to pay!' the fork hit the kitchen table with some force. My jaw followed suit and dropped down to my chest as I watched this action play out. The fork bounced off the table and up towards the hair on Patience's head - landing in the middle of her head, SCREAM! The fork was stuck! Only milliseconds had passed. SCREAM, as Patience swept her hand up to her head to pull at the fork. SCREAMS as her hand found the blood - as if we needed more evidence of this awful accident playing out! She dragged her bloodied hand down the kitchen wall, leaving a horrific mark and confirmation we needed to do more. Alan looked me in the eye and casually remarked, "Don't know what happened there I was aiming for the wall."

At this time, I was still talking to the council about the bill; calmly I questioned "A and E then?" - and off we went. After that we breathed, there was quiet, much needed quiet and the visits stopped.

It is important to reflect that God places people in front of us for a reason, if only for a week, a season, or a year. Each one is there to either offer help or to be helped. We need to be asking ourselves wwwww: what, why, where, when, who. What is God teaching me, why now, where is this leading, when will I act and who is the person?

This was by no means the end of Patience, the initial opportunity that God gave to her, continued to open my front door. We became lengthy May Flies, together through lows and highs and when the advice and words became too close for the truth we would drift and breathe in the silence. Time passed in the shape of a few years and then there were two. The baby came along and there were many tears; the dad stayed for a season, then went his own way. We stayed for two seasons, the emotions of parenthood and the expectations on me were too high. It was such a challenging time for all that I am sure my forgetfulness to meet with God and to pray did not help that situation. I had no accountability partner, (a Christian friend who could pray with me, talk things through from the Lords perspective) and our own family had grown also. I knew that this time, if Patience and I parted it would be for good we would not be breathing but holding our breaths. It was with bated breath and the foulest of language that we went our separate ways.

I was not expecting to hear her name in conversation in our home again, her leaving a few years before was still raw. After all, how often can we keep on forgiving? 'As often as I do' is what my Lord keeps on telling me. It is the hardest thing to do, but the right thing is always the hardest thing to do. As a family we were at mid crisis point when Patience got in touch with her concerns. She had gone through my daughter Cherrie, via social media. This was a gesture as my daughter holds a grudge; she had mastered holding a grudge to post grad level. For Patience to reach out and for Cherrie to take her hand, it should paint enough of a picture as to the crisis we were in. But Patience's story is not a platform for the crisis, that will have its own chapter later. What the crisis had done was create yet another opportunity for her to come back into our lives. Her daughter was now 3 and struggling with varying needs, Patience needed support and I was back to WWWWW. It was clear that God wanted me to help. If I am honest, I was reluctant as Patience still found it so hard to listen and to act on clear advice. Any word spoken, texted or breathed was always a dig. Patience has always struggled to see only love from my intentions and this creates a toxic relationship, as every action is questioned and pulled apart.

Then it occurred to me how selfish I am. You see we all have a skill set, that skill set is from God. God places that skill set there, as part of the gifts he has given to us. Who am I to refuse the use of that gift towards a person I believe God had placed before me? Regardless of our current crisis, my Father God, all those years ago, had placed Patience directly onto our path. Now I was skilled up and better informed to support her, and so we breathed again.

We continue to keep on trying. We have been blessed with lessons from Patience for nineteen years and the years will continue, as we no longer breathe apart from each other. We both have grown so much; God placed Patience at my door and that has placed these words in my heart.

Philippians 1:6.

'And I am certain that God, who began the good work within you, will continue his work until it is finally finished on the day when Christ Jesus returns.

So it is right that I should feel as I do about all of you, for you have a special place in my heart.'

2
RED

I unexpectedly received a call from our local School of English, asking if we could help them out.

I was unsure initially with their recruiting methods and then with our own ability to manage another child in our life, albeit for the summer. Nick felt that we had been given an opportunity to bring culture to our home. He arrived out of the London taxi with a bottle bright head of intense red hair. It was ironic, as Cherrie was upstairs with the exact same colour and length of hair on her head. Fortunately, hers was a blessing, as we had that same week, been for an interview for the sixth form Performing Arts course at our local grammar school. A traditional grammar school that stresses in bold in the student handbook that students must not dye their hair. So, it was with trepidation that we entered the interview to fight for this sixth form place. Now we need to remember that in all things God is in control and before we even reach tomorrow, He has already left His footprint. At that time, I had faith and I would have said I knew Jesus, although I did not have enough faith that Jesus could secure a sixth form place. I placed pressure on my daughter to try and wash the colour out of her hair - she who encouraged each of her children to embrace their unique identity was calling out 'Use more fairy liquid, it will help it fade.'

Yet I was sporting a full head of purple streaks in my own hair! I really felt that the Grammar School place took priority over my beliefs and that we needed to do what we could to secure it. This was strange as I remember being really fixed on this place for my daughter, yet my usual stance is No SATs, No Kent tests, do not measure children on their ability on one given day.

The school office was small, I felt awkward sitting with my daughter having her grades discussed and her work ethic - not that Cherrie had a poor work ethic. She had come from the local school with low outcomes and was often referred to as 'the school for unmarried mothers'. Being at the Grammar School amongst such high achieving parents, I felt, as we sat in the interview room, that we were the children left at the back of the class. As every other child is picked for the team apart from you and your friend. There was a knock at the office door and another teacher walked in, introduced herself as Head of Performing Arts, looked at my daughter and asked, ' Are you keeping the hair?' I started to fumble for the right excuse when my daughter firmly said yes. To which the teacher explained they were performing Grease in sixth form and needed a Frenchie, 'Your hair will fit that role nicely.' I am sure that the offer of a place at sixth form was based on Cherrie's grades and work ethic, however it could be debated as no sooner did sixth form start, Cherrie was offered the role of Frenchie.

There we were, standing on the pavement with Red from Slovenia, my first foreign student. He had just turned 13 and liked science fiction, this was all his profile gave me. I am continuously reminded by my family that when I am talking to anyone who does not speak English, not to over gesture or over sign each word that 1 speak. This reminder was because of this moment with Red. He climbed out of the taxi and I walked towards him with my hubby behind me and said 'Wer... el... Co... Oom... e to our home.' as I got to the word home, I was drawing in the air with my hands, the shape of a house. I must have looked like a mad woman, poor boy must have thought, 'Really, I have to spend my holiday with this mad woman?' Thankfully Red ignored me and aimed towards my husband Nick who had his hand outstretched for a handshake. 'Hello' said Red in perfect English. I mean it was better than mine and Nick's put together and so started our first experience of being a Host family. I imagined my role to be one of a Mother who nurtures and role models while supporting Red with his English lessons. I was keen to impress and ready to be fully involved, getting up early to set up breakfast and knocking on Red's door at 7am. Then I knocked again at eight, then nine and at 1pm. He finally showed his face at about half past one, we sat and ate lunch and he explained he really did not need to be in school; he had a point but this was his spoken English, his written English was another matter. I agreed his English was good and suggested we try for a school day tomorrow.

I thought about how to occupy a thirteen-year-old from a foreign country who likes science fiction, so I introduced Red to Doctor Who, New Who to be precise, the rebooted version from 2005 onwards. This was the making of Red's time with us, however Red did not attend any lessons that summer, or pass any exams.

Red remained glued to the TV and the Internet for all thing's Dr Who. You can imagine his delight when we found time to chat about the originals and the spin offs! Red also got on so well with Alan and Cherrie, my eldest two children. As a family we had not travelled abroad which is why I wanted to make the world smaller for them by hosting students. I have a house of autistic young people and travelling anywhere is not something we do, autism is about processing the sensory, the physical, the emotional, everything is heightened including daily living. It is not that you cannot go out, it's more about taking longer to do what other people do so quickly. You need strategies in place to do the simplest of daily tasks and continuous reminders. The thought of going somewhere else is terrifying, not predictable, and therefore avoided at all costs. Not dissimilar to being on the outside lane of a motorway at 70 miles an hour with traffic speeding around you and your engine stops, you have broken down! All that fear, totally unexpected and out of your control.

It was lovely to see Red, Alan and Cherrie get on so well, providing an opportunity for Red to broaden his vocabulary in the local vernacular, which he did. This led me to tell Red a new truth or lie, namely, when you want to pass on your love and kindness and gratitude to someone you say Spaz Monkey. A common word frequently used by those who live in Kent. Well, that is what the children told Red and while he stayed at our home, he would frequently call out 'Spaz Monkey' to all of us.

When he left to travel home, he took his love for Dr Who, the ability to swear in fifteen different languages and the words Spaz Monkey. For me at that time, I had not thought of the experience God had given me with Red, yet when I look at all the people through our door, none of them planned, it gives thought to James 4:13-14:

"Look here, you who say, "Today or tomorrow we are going to a certain town and will stay there a year. We will do business there and make a profit." How do you know what your life will be like tomorrow? Your life is like the morning fog—it's here a little while, then it's gone".

I had no idea how that very moment of meeting Red was going to turn out, I did have a clear idea of my role as a host family. Yet this was not meant to be. It was not the journey we were to have with him or him with us. Instead, for that summer, we had a young man in our home who became a family member. We experienced life in Slovenia through the stories Red shared and he embraced our uniqueness as much as we did him. Then he was gone, well almost. When he was fifteen, he came back to stay. I was so excited to meet him again and to see how he had grown. Red was now a young adult; he was embracing life, taking risks as many teens do as well as all his meals in his room. By week four when he went home, I felt deflated and aware that we cannot look back and try to recreate things that have passed. On pushing the door to his bedroom, it became stuck. On pushing again, the crockery bounced together, and I was in. The room was a scene from 'How clean is tour house?' Plates full of food, food in the floorboards, mold on the food, food in the bed. Take out pots and packets under pillows, under the bed, stuffed behind furniture. We do not know what tomorrow will bring, but there is no point trying to plan or control it, our Father wants the best for us and that is all that matters, for the day is soon gone. It vanishes just as some people do from our lives, but their story always remains.

I am reminded that Christ calls us to be Christians, He knows we are only human and we make mistakes. He wants us to forget what has gone before, not to dwell in the past but to move forward to the goal that awaits; by doing this we will grow in faith and grow in role modelling Christ the best way that we can.

Philippians 3:13–14

No, dear brothers and sisters, I have not achieved it, but I focus on this one thing: Forgetting the past and looking forward to what lies ahead, I press on to reach the end of the race and receive the heavenly prize for which God, through Christ Jesus, is calling us.

How is your Faith?
Journal here!

†

3
SORELLO

Sorello means sister and this is who she quickly became.

We were not surprised that Sorello was beautiful, the daughter of a well-respected Italian English teacher who had come to stay for the summer. Sorello had stunning ebony long curly hair, a pale complexion and dark eyes which lit up when she laughed. Sorello laughed a lot, delighting us all with her beautiful nature and compassionate ways. She supported her mother taking students on trips while her mother also taught lessons, no surprise then that her English was perfect. She fitted into the family as if she were the missing piece that we did not know we needed until she arrived. Sorello was organised, always busy, and over time placed on the extra daughter list as Patience had been before.

Of course, hosting students generally occurred in the summertime which was conveniently after the latest season of Doctor Who. So began our efforts to ensure we had educated all our students with our great British culture. Sorello was no different and she threw herself in into it all. In all honestly, I am not sure if Sorello enjoyed Dr Who, but she had a beautiful heart and responded with smiles and laughter and fear at all the right given moments in each scene, delighting my younger children. After all sharing something with a close friend, is in comparison like giving a piece of yourself away. You worry that there may be judgement, you fear the response and wait with bated breath that the relationship is still okay and not in jeopardy. This worry is not good and with God's grace I do not hold these worries at all anymore. Steven Furtick discussed this type of response beautifully with:

Eclesiastés 11:4

"Farmers who wait for perfect weather never plant. If they watch every cloud, they never harvest".

This is not about daydreaming but about whether we watch the wind, watch, and worry what other people think, what other people see in us. Spending our time responding to pleasing others over pleasing God, judging others but justifying it by saying you would say it to their face, watching the wind.

Whilst there are many moments that sit in my heart, they are not all for sharing, you will get distracted and lean over for the chocolate, crisps or wine. Either way the precious moments of mundane life are special for each individual but boring to others who do not know you well. So, I will tell you that the passionate Italians you hear about exist but experiencing this passion and reading about it in books, are two vastly different things.

Sorello visited for several consecutive summers and was now 18. I had a strict open-door policy in my home, meaning that all the doors in the house stay open, this had been in place since the beginning of time, mainly because it's important to keep an ear out for children and their squabbles but also because you want to hear if they suddenly call out. The spare room which houses all our Father's guests was in the attic. Sometimes it moved depending on the needs of the family at each given time, but it has never been empty since we have lived here. It's nothing much to look at - Nick and I are no DIY experts. Our home is freshened up once every ten years with a lick of paint but even then, the paintwork in the hallway has never been done, and it is tired and passes for vintage and distressed now. The room is bright and cosy, yet no matter where the double bed goes, you do need to climb over the bed to access drawers or boxes on the other side. In the words of the great Stephen Fry, 'it is compact and bijou.' Though it is a room that holds forgiveness. While you might curse as you knock your head on the eves as you fit the sheet on the bed, you would not change this little room. It has a tiny balcony that has just enough space to place a small burnt orange mosaic round table and accompanying chair. The Victorian Street sits below and the Carnegie library which has kept these Town houses company since they were built, it is just on your right and shares the same address. In November there is a wonderful view of the harbour fireworks above the rooftops and in December you can clearly see the Father Christmas search lights, which look for his sleigh on the countdown to Our Lord's birthday. In spring we have sat and witnessed the starlings flitting across the clear evening sky in their synchronised flight. If luck is with you, you may witness the burnt orange of bushy tails flying past, as the local foxes race by in the late hours or dusky mornings, shopping in the neighbouring bins for treats and tastes to feed their cubs. Once and only once the small black ball of a bat shot past our faces as we sat in our moonlit garden on our wedding night.

It was May, there was a cloudless sky and birds sang out their joyful tunes. Standing on the balcony there was a sense of anticipation and of all good things, as this dear old town went about its daily business.

Sorello was in the balcony room and her friend, Georgeio, was up there with her. I was not aware of trouble until it came knocking at the door in the form of Victoria, Sorello's mother.

'Let me in!' Victoria shouted as she banged the brass knocker on the door. 'Let me in, she has a boy, she has a boy in her room!'

My children were eating in the kitchen. I have no recollection of the time off day that Victoria called, but I am sure it must have been in the evening. It says something about our home when your children just accept the random craziness that goes on. This is in part due to my mother's costume walk enactments. She would stand on our top step every summer, a few evenings a month, in a Victorian dress and straw bonnet. Portraying the grand lady from number 7, as an expectant audience, a group of usually fifteen or more on lookers, stood in the road. My mother would walk cautiously down the steps, the reason being that she had lost her eyesight at the age of 34. She walked with care because she was registered blind and never liked to act this short scene with her cane.

Losing her sight did not stop her from embracing all the Challenges life gave her. She raised money for St George's church by driving round Brands Hatch and travelling to London with Tom to take her place on the Blue Peter set with her Blue Peter Guide Dog, Fergie. Playing the grand lady living at number 7 was a role she enjoyed, declaring in the street about the man who built the houses on the lawn and how he swindled the owners. This short monologue re-lived the history that played out two hundred years ago.

I digress; my children responded with 'meh' when I explained it might get loud as Victoria was angry and we were going to sort this out the best we could.

Sorello was mid step on the stairs by now, apologising and crying while Victoria was still banging and shouting at the door. I put my hand on the latch, took a deep breath, and opened the door.

Victoria pushed the door with full force so that it bounced off the hall wall behind and banged shut. Victoria had landed and wanted Georgio's head, but to get to him she had to get past Sorello! Unfortunately, I have never been any good at languages and so am unable to tell you what was expressed on my stairs, but it was powerful and full of protest. Both mother and daughter were heading in full force to the attic room, the speed of speech was incredible and somehow poetic. I was leading the rear and trying my best to remind Victoria that Sorello was eighteen and that indoor voices are best. This was a mistake as Victoria burst into more Italian with her arms waving all over the place as if directing traffic. Georgio had sensibly placed himself in my daughter's doorway; as they reached him, he joined in with the Italian debate the velocity of the voices played out as if a Greek tragedy was being performed on the tiny landing! The passionate voices began to move, three bodies sharing and heading down two sets of stairs, it was a miracle nobody fell. I followed trying to calm everyone down, Georgio took the lead as all three shouting Italians moved to the front door, then Georgio was gone, having smoothly sneaked out of the front door. One down two to go; I was left with mother and daughter still shouting. I understood Victoria was extremely concerned for her daughter, but for any relationship to grow and develop we need to trust and in that moment at that time there was no trust there. Sorello was in tears, I remember my heart crying out for her. My daughter came up and announced there was no need to understand languages as it was clear by the voices and tones that what was said was not nice. We felt as we had been hit by a hurricane, this forceful Italian mother protecting her young, this is one passionate lady whom you would want to keep on your side for all battles.

This brings me to our Father, as you need to know He will fight all our battles and displays equal wrath to that of Victoria, however this type of wrath is seen In the Old Testament. In the New Testament we see unconditional love, our Father delights in the spiritual growth we make and in times of trouble He offers out His arms and carries us.

Psalm 2:12

"Submit to God's royal son, or he will become angry, and you will be destroyed in the midst of all your activities for his anger flares up in an instant." But what joy for all who take refuge in him!

Many Ministers, Vicars, Pastors and Evangelist, will tell us that it is entirely up to us what type of relationship we have with God; we have that choice to build trust and to care what our Father thinks. Reading scripture daily is one of the ways to build a relationship with God and like any good parent, our Father will guide us and provide for us with what we need, but not always what we want. When we feel far away from God, so alone and forgotten, we need to remember that this is of our own making. We make decisions to put earthly rituals in our way, we get pulled in our soap operas, reality TV, social media, smoking, drinking, shopping and so the list goes on. We choose to stay away from God and sit in virtual escape rooms where we lose account of time and sight of what is precious.

The consequences of moving away from God are not dissimilar to the consequences of not laying down firm foundations of trust in our relationships with our family and friends. We experience total breakdown, we become spiritually dead and left not knowing how to repair the damage. Be at ease because God loves us so much, He is willing to become the center of our lives despite how distracted we are, He loves us unconditionally and through Him we can do all things.

How does God lift you up?
Journal here!

†

4
PARLEY

Parley means to discuss with an enemy, holding a conference with the opposing side. I am sure it will become clear why this chap has this name.

It was a beautiful early June day when the local school of English telephoned asking me to take a one-week emergency placement, of course I was happy to help. There was a moment of panic when I remembered that I had left Christmas unpacked in the spare room, with banners and baubles everywhere. The spare room had become a fairy grotto as I felt comfortable that I had till the spring to make a move to clear it out. Not much more to say about that, as you all know that feeling of surprise and disbelief at how quickly the seasons pass. It felt like a moment ago that we sat and celebrated Jesus's birthday and now here we were in June!

Parley stood on my doorstep, over 6ft and as broad as the doorway. He had travelled from Dubai to study English so he could attend university like his brothers and take an engineering degree. I explained to him as he dragged his trunk that he was staying for one week only. I had no Google translate so my arms were drawing pictures in the air to back up my verbal instructions. 'Es Es Es', he mumbled? as we made our way upstairs. It was 9.30 in the morning and no sooner had we reached the attic room than Parley dropped his trunk and laid himself out on the bed. His broad shoulders and long legs filled the space, much like the character Gulliver in Lilliput, he made the room feel miniature as if it were a doll's house. I felt relieved that this was only for one week. The bed needed reinforcing, the floor needed twice as much space to hold the heavy trunk and I was fearful the balcony would cave in with the weight of the tall gentleman before me.

I stood for a while watching this man laid out on the bed, gently breathing, then realised he had fallen asleep. That was it, this is easy I thought, no meals to cook, nothing. I had not seen Parley for over twenty-four hours. School had been informed but as he was an adult and he had been in touch with his father there was no need for me to worry. Then he came home, clutching three Kentucky family buckets, his dark eyes mostly closed behind the top bucket which hid half of his face. Nick, my husband, looked him up and down and declared as if I had never seen the like, that he had a serious case of the munchies! I knew this, I knew teenagers. I also knew my ex-hubby very well, and realised that Parley was stoned. It was two in the afternoon when Parley came downstairs, I was washing the kitchen floor on my hands and knees, he came in sat down and said, ' Your life is shit,' got up and went back to his room.

Parleys' waking hours were from midnight to about ten in the morning, he then slept, woke up for a drink at about two in the afternoon and slept again till the house had gone to bed. He was no real bother, did not like English, home cooked meals, women cleaning, daylight, but always interacted beautifully with my eldest Alan and smiled wide beams at the younger children. He always dressed well and had excellent personal hygiene - which is saying something after Red! He hardly spoke, bought take-out meals most days which he preferred to eat out on the small balcony,and then would infuse the air with his partaking off the natural hemp plant. Any time Parley saw me cleaning he told me that my life was shit. I might remind you that Parley was only staying with us for a fleeing moment, a taxi was being sent over to pick him up that Friday and his short stay would end. Friday arrived and I tried to explain to

Parley that he needed to pack as his stay with us was now over and his original host family were now home. Parley waved his arms and then turned to look at the balcony and announced, 'No I stay'. I telephoned the school who told me they would send a translator, which they did. I waited downstairs in the kitchen, passing time wiping down the cupboards. Parley came in with the translator, looked at me and stated again that my life was shit. He then smiled and told me he was staying. The translator explained that Parley needed to pass his English and was booked to stay for one year. His father owned many businesses internationally and this was Parley's opportunity to study and join the family business.

It was settled, Parley was staying and for the first six months he partied, smoked, ate huge amounts of take out and rarely went to school. Every so often he would sit in the kitchen and question me in a style I had always thought was unique to Yoda from Star Wars.

"Jacqueline pass English, will I?" I would look directly into his dark eyes; between the floppy fringe he carried so well and repeat my answer from the week before.

'When you study and go to school you will pass'.

Parley would then laugh aloud and pat my shoulder and say, 'One day...' He then continued life as before, well liked, sociable, kind and fun. Always out with all the short stay students, with my son Alan and never learnt English.

Then the dark day arrived, I found Parley with his head in his hands, his father was coming over and he needed to pass two exams to measure his progress and to be able to finish the year out. I am not sure what I expected to happen, but I did not expect the complete turnaround that I saw. Parley got up for breakfast the following morning, ate and left for school, he came home with homework which he asked for help to complete. He even stayed and chatted and ate evening meals with us. This new routine saw immediate improvement in his English, the measure of improvement was recorded and Parley stayed till the end of the year. I would love to say that this turn around continued and he passed with flying colours. I know Parley managed to improve and went home relieved, but it was not the outcome his parents hoped for.

When I re-live Parley's stay with us, this short account in no way reflects the year. I had been supporting the church with a discipleship class. One autistic chap of whom I am particularly fond, had been trying to get his life on track since I met him at Alpha. Each year he wanted to do better, and all the time he came to church and listened to God's word, spending time with his church family, we witnessed improvement. Then he would get caught up in life's distractions, after all we are only human, but it is at this point each year that we would lose sight of our dear friend. When Parley, settled down to a positive routine and took the nurture on offer to him he began to thrive. God can only help us if we continually seek Him and ask Him for his help and guidance; read his word and where possible seek wise counsel from a trusted person. Better still ask that trusted person to be your accountability partner; I asked Tracy, and whilst since asking we have cried and prayed a thousand times, and sometimes found ourselves being sent in directions we were resistant to; Tracy has kept me grounded in God's word. Allowing decisions to be Jesus focused and action taken with a sense of peace about them, despite how difficult some of the choices have been.

27 Luke

"And so I tell you, keep on asking, and you will receive what you ask for. Keep on seeking, and you will find. Keep on knocking, and the door will be opened to you.

We said to our dear ASD friend last night, keep calling in, we can help you and support you if you are here. If we do not see you, we are useless. Our Father and Creator needs to see us. He needs to hear from us, to know our anxious hearts, our hopes and dreams and it's the honest truth that God has the biggest dreams for us. He created you, you are so special to Him that He listens to every thought that passes through your mind - He breathed the very life into you. So of course, He wants the absolute best for you. Yet still this amount of love and care is pointless if we do not see Him and place our lives into His outreached hands.

Notes
Journal here!

5
IVY

I magine the plant and then you can imagine Ivy who arrived liked a storm with a need to stay.

Some blood ties are like that and those who are connected to family by other means can be equally demanding. Ivy was part of the old life I had with my ex, so I was surprised that she telephoned looking for a room. I was stuck with a closed throat as the words were pushed out from my voice box.

'Yes of course, it will be fun'. A small part of me felt it might be. After all, the children were here and there was a history and genetic disposition on their father's side. You kind of hope for something to click, but the only sound I often heard was the sucked in breath from the pursed lips of my hubby Nick. The stay was only supposed to be for ten days and therefore manageable. However, the visit came with family drama and I discovered quickly that I was the center of that drama – because nobody on Keith's side believed Cherrie was his daughter despite all the obvious genetic evidence.

I know - what do you do with that knowledge? After all, no matter what I knew of conception and creation, people who did not know me well had reached their own conclusions to a matter that did not concern them. Made their own case without even allowing me a say in the matter. A verdict was reached without inviting me to the trial, which from what Ivy told me was based on idle chit chat and everyone, including Ivy, believed it.

It seems appropriate to speak about Psalm 139 and my first daughter. I had Alan when I was 22, he was a total surprise and challenged every inch of my bones to the core, emotionally and physically, but I loved him so much. This screaming crying chunky boy was delightful on a good day and I strongly believed would be better off with a sibling. Keith, however, was reeling with the shock of his first born and unbeknown to me Keith was also turning to eye other women. For me though, I loved Keith wholeheartedly; if he needed a kidney, I was the person that would let him have mine. I believed marriage was created in church in the eyes of God, Keith believed marriage was for sharing. I prayed and planned and on the right day with the right timing, Keith and I shared a moment and I fell pregnant for our second child;

> Psalm 139: 13-15
>
> 'You made all the delicate, inner parts of my body and knit me together in my mother's womb. Thank you for making me so wonderfully complex!
>
> Your workmanship is marvelous—how well I know it. You watched me as I was being formed in utter seclusion, as I was woven together in the dark of the womb".

Cherrie was so meant to be, I saw her as mine and not Keith's. Mainly because I was not the only girl Keith was making up to and this kept him busy elsewhere. I spent a lot of time parenting Alan and Cherrie on my own so they became mine, very much. Especially Cherrie, planned to the second and given by the Grace of God, I was not to know what a saving grace she would be till much later. To return to Ivy, to be honest I am not that keen to unpack this one, but I pray it will be cathartic. On this visit Ivy was more self-important than in the past. Cherrie was now of an age where she was going to need help with university and Ivy was going to offer her the means to manage her studies and to get the grades she needed, without holding down two jobs. Cherrie was also going to be entitled to a sum of money when Ivy was no longer here; if she obeyed the rules attached, Cherrie could look forward to being comfortable financially. The rules it turned were clear:

"Do not help or support your mother, and do not give her monetary gifts".

"Do not party at university and do not spend your days doing what other teens do."

Between each sentence Ivy lit a cigarette, we are in the days when smoking in the home was considered normal. The smoke trickled through the house and curled its way over and into furniture, curtains, bedding, and ceilings lights, just as her words were doing. My home had a stale yellow tinge to it and Ivy announced she had more business to complete while she was here and would stay longer!

Some people are just oblivious, they truly believe that their words are kind and that their actions are in the best interest of those they impact on, but the truth is they are superficial and only God sees their real heart. So, there we were, the conditions to being comfortable were outlined to Cherrie and in response to this Cherrie exploded,

'How dare you believe I am the type of person who would refuse to help my mother? How dare you after never supporting or visiting Alan and I, think that this is okay? I am not interested in anything you may have'. Then it came, the lecture, 'You can have all this and be someone, but I expect you to come out at least once a year, fly over'.

'Well' said my daughter, 'I would rather be the person my mum has made me to be than anything you have in mind.'

The smoke encircled Ivy's face and her mouth, being slightly opened, meant it also fell from her parted lips like dry ice in a budget cult film set in a church yard. Ivy had met her match and broken her last promise, you would think after upsetting the harmony she would leave, instead she stayed the summer. It was costly, awkward and heart breaking for my daughter and the first real understanding that family is not always the people connected by blood but those you choose.

I have no idea what Keith had said to Ivy to instill such a strange belief, but the heart knows what it knows. Cherrie is Keith's and I guess the one moment she had with her paternal grandfather reinforced this. Her biological grandfather had got in touch and it was all very strange. His son Keith had been adopted illegally and he had been trying to track his children for some time. He shared the family tree with Cherrie, and she spent a few hours looking at old photographs he shared, and you could not deny the family resemblance. Again, Cherrie knew who her dad was, but I worried about the idea that the family believed she was not her father's child. (I had spent far too much time watching the wind). The time Keith I had had together was great; we loved with such passion, but he smoked natural grown grass with equal passion. He was chilled twenty-four seven, sometimes not even remembering to have a meal, or what arrangements he had made. I had stopped smoking everything but became paranoid that I had missed a memory. Had a drink been spiked, was there an immaculate conception that I failed to notice, did I miss the angel's visit completely? I do not jest; I have always been 'scatty', forgetful and in a complete muddle most days. I struggled to be organized; managing life as well as my peers was not ever going to be easy for me. Life was haphazard and often complicated. I was highly anxious and missed social cues all the time, but it was clear when we visited Cherrie's biological grandfather that all was well with the world and I could stop worrying.

What Ivy gave to me was a valuable gift, as I saw the unconditional love of Christ reflected in my daughter's heart. I saw clearly that the Pharisees from Jesus' time still exists today and still try to infect others with what they believe is right and true. We need to be armed and prepared as we are vulnerable to the materialistic world we live in, as propaganda shapes what we spend. The pull of money has broken many lives, ripping hearts in two and leaving most of the world's population in extreme poverty. Often it starts with someone placing conditions and value on things and the need to control becomes overpowering.

This is not what God offers us, He says He loves us unconditionally just as we are and I will take that love with a good dose of hardship any day; and "my bones will sing His praise," to quote a beautiful song.

What is your relationship with Christ?
Journal here!

†

6
BELLE

Her name needs no explanation, just think of sparkles and all things Disney.

If you don't have a close relationship with God yet then you need to know that He sends you the right people at the right time; you know deep inside by the connection you make with them that they have been sent by God. The reason may not be too clear, it has taken me a lifetime to realise that this house and the unexpected guests have been sent by God, to equip me for my work to serve. I have learnt so much, gained new skills, developed emotionally in ways I never thought possible. In the words of a great song: "God is so good to me." Belle was sent into my life at the right time. From the moment she was born I was there; I needed the focus of this tiny beautiful precious babe; then later she came back to me and it had such a positive impact at a difficult time.

Proverbs 3:5-6

"Trust in the LORD with all your heart; do not depend on your own understanding. Seek his will in all you do, and he will show you which path to take."

This speaks about how we need to trust in God, and that we should not lean on our human thoughts. The visual of this is good to work with, as when we lean, we move from a upright position that is sturdy, we stand on solid ground. We slant our bodies and suddenly we are not so sure if we can maintain the balance. When I lean on my human thoughts and doubt my father, I have never found myself to be in a good place.

Imagine you are in a space that is only yours, that this space can be as big or as small as you like, as warm or as cold as you wish. You can fill this space with whatever you wish. It can be outside in the country, a room, or a holiday memory. Shut your eyes and feel the space, let the space you have created heighten your senses. Feel the skip of your heartbeat as the excitement of exploring this place and developing this space fills you from within. There is a sense of fulfilment that everything is fine and for this moment alone all is well. This picture I have painted is Belle. Belle carried with her a sense of calm, she is was organised and motivated and arrived in my house much like Mary Poppins. Belle was God's plan and my eldest niece though only 14 years younger than me. We were of an age where we were friends and the Aunt had been removed. In fact, I don't think the Aunt role was ever really there except perhaps when she tiny, when I held her hand as she balanced on walls, or ran along the sands with her as we jumped to break up the sandcastle we had made. For Belle, I think I was always her grown up friend, for me Belle was the grounding I held onto as my teenage world fell apart.

Belle arrived out of sorts and out of the blue, even in this disheveled state she carried a Disney princess quality about her. No sooner had she unpacked her belongings into the spare room than we all felt better prepared for whatever lay ahead.

Belle had left university and felt lost and needed time to take stock. She had contacted me and so of course Nick drove the three hundred odd miles to pick her up. You do not ask questions from those you trust; you just act. Belle has a simply wonderful manner about her and her love for people and organising those around her meant that those she met really did feel listened to and valued.

The whole event was perfect timing, for Cherrie had finally an older sister role model. This meant Alan had some space from Cherrie, although it also meant that Alan had two strong females to battle with and not a high chance of winning. This did not go down to well with Alan although it was a small price to pay for the balance of wellbeing. Do not get me wrong, Alan won many house debates. Whether he was right or wrong, he would always bring forward a solid argument and the extra wit from Belle for these moments, were a delight to watch or listen to. Jonathon now had someone new to relate to, not that he did not know Belle, as he had seen her when we visited my sister up north. However, Jonathon's days passed by in a haze. He admits that a lot that went on, pre-fourteen, is just a blur. Jonathon struggled when he was young not just with ill health but with autism. People were a no-go area and just added confusion to his life. So, to manage and build on new social skills, we needed to introduce people to Jonathon in the home, where life was safe and held its routine, which is why we had students.

While Belle's arrival threw him off balance, the structure she bought with her was life changing for the time she was here. Gertie-Grace benefited the best I think from Belle's arrival, you need to remember the Disney princess qualities Belle effortlessly displayed. Gertie-Grace was an engaging toddler with lots of unusual quirks and she only related to people once she knew them. Belle was her cousin and loved all things pink and girlie so within a month everything Gertie-Grace owned was pink or lilac; meal times were full of sparkles and Belle had settled in.

The wonders of having Belle to stay I am sure worked both ways. It was not long before she started to relax, felt emotionally well, and made plans. This started with a job at our local pub, waitressing. On days when Belle was home, she mucked in and helped and when it became a challenge for me to balance school events with nursery and work commitments, Belle stepped in. One of these 'stepping in' days was to support Jonathon on a school trip on Roman Day. He was seven years old at the time and to be honest does not remember much about this event except for Belle having the best toga and looking like a real lady from Rome. In the world of seven-year old's, there is sense of importance when you are the best.

Belle also was able to reduce the help I required from my mother on Great Ormond Street days. No longer did I have to ask mum to babysit the long day we were away. Instead, Belle happily stepped in and saw us off and looked after Cherrie and Alan, spending much needed one to one girlie time with Cherrie, while Alan saw his dad. I understand from Cherrie that these days were her most formative years, sharing seasons of Sex in the City while eating meal deals and online shopping. Now I am sure all of you will have an opinion on Sex in the city, but Belle did ask permission and Cherrie has always been older than her years, growing up as a young carer and then as older sister to three siblings. Having said that, please know that Cherrie was about fourteen at the time and some life learning with your favourite cousin really can be just what is needed for solid grounding and foundation building.

On one of these GOSH visits, Jonathon was beside himself, he did not want to go, he struggled with huge social anxieties, ate little, felt constant pain, did not sleep and the break in routine was crippling for him. To get him into the car we always took Cheesy the bear - the bears are another story. Bears are expensive, but not in charity shops. To manage shopping excursions and any other trip out, Jonathon and I would look for bears in charity shop windows and rescue them. He had over thirty bears on the bottom bunk of is bed and Cheesy was the best bear. 'Cheesy is a naked bear,' said Belle to Jonathon. 'What he needs is a waistcoat. As he is a smart clever bear, I will make Cheesy a waistcoat for your return'. So 'Cheesy' stayed behind and we took Buzz Light Year instead, leaving Belle with the task of creating a bear waistcoat.

Once we had finished the routine checks at GOSH we wanted to get back home. I was always lethargic from travel pills on these days and my bed was calling me. Jonathon had already had his fries, for which he had finally got a taste. That is the thing you see, when you have a child, whose diet is restricted and they discover a liking for a new food, you just go with it. I had done the 'no pudding till the plate is empty' game with Alan and Cherrie and to be honest all it creates is tension and trauma at the dinner table. Having Jonathon with so many different issues when he was small, had taught me a different way of parenting and both Nick and I had shifted our priorities. Belle telephoned for an eta, asking us to go via Ashford which would lengthen our journey slightly, giving her enough time to finish the waistcoat. Jonathon was asleep in the car, so a detour was not a problem. On arriving home, Belle, Alan, and Cherrie were all waiting for us on the top step. Alan helped unload the various bags we had taken, and Cherrie came to get her brother. In her hand, she held a very smart blue waist coated bear which Jonathon immediately took and held onto tightly.

Belle look harassed and unkempt which was a first and she told me sewing on short notice and with time restrictions was 'definitely' not her thing!

Painting, I discovered that summer, was her thing. We had been sitting in her room and chatted about how tired it was looking, and I announced, without really thinking of budget that we should decorate. Belle got overly excited and wanted to paint the furniture as well as the room. We decided to look at what we had in the shed first and found some mint green and lilac paint. That was that then, the room would have lilac walls with mint green on the window wall. We would paint the tired brown furniture white and change the bedding and pictures on the wall. Neither of us planned any further that, you do not when money and time is tight. We just carried the furniture into the garden, grabbed some brushes and started to paint. James our neighbour looked over the wall. I think there was moment in Belle's stay with us that he may have had romantic thoughts towards her, but today he just beamed and asked what we were up to. What you must understand is that James was refurbishing his first house project. He was talented and able and had OCD, so everything was done with a perfect finish. Here was Belle and I slapping on paint with no prime coat, no sanding down and not any masking tape! Poor chap cringed from across the fence and stated that this was Blue Peter and not painting! James maybe right, we were not the best painters but the room makeover we did that day lasted ten years and served a purpose of welcoming many other guests to our home.

Belles' talents meant she soon found herself work in administration at a specialist school and from there she applied for a job as cabin crew on Easy Jet.

Nearer the time to Belle leaving, we were out having lunch at the local pub when an elderly gypsy lady came from nowhere and placed her hand on Belles hand. 'I see a baby boy', she said and walked out of the pub. I looked Belle directly in the eyes and she firmly stated.

'No, No, No I am not pregnant! Anyway, I am not with Chris anymore, I left work to meet him for lunch and realised we have different priorities.'

'How did you realise that?' I asked.

'It was the skateboard, he turned up on and the half dozen mates he bought with him, not what I want from a 24-year-old! Belle continued to travel back and forth from London when she started work with Easy Jet, then rented a room nearer to the airport. The following Christmas was quiet and I must admit it was less organised than the previous one, when Belle was here. Though we did clear away a lot quicker; this was because Belle was incredibly slow at eating and while we had all finished and pulled crackers, adorning the table with colourful crepe paper and our heads with equally bright coloured hats, Belle would still be eating. While we raced penguins between empty wine glasses and over makeshift gravy boat slaloms, Belle would still be on turkey and roast potatoes, which is fine; of course its fine, until your bottom hurts and you just want to drift away, just as the children and grandparents had done!

Christmas without Belle there to share the fun, was not going to be same, the smaller details that make up the difference between thought out and sparkles, is Belle. I knew I would miss her greatly, so it was an easy decision to make when I discovered I was pregnant to ask her to be God mother. Yes Belle, the lady was right you were to have a baby boy in your life soon. I might add here that Nick and I had been told after Jonathon was born that we could not conceive, but that is another story and we know God is so good to us.

When Belle joined Easy Jet, she added her sparkle there and then added it to Virgin. We were so proud of her red coat and she had worked hard to get it. During this time Belle met her Disney prince, not through her travelling but a simple blind date type thing, a friend of a friend. We were thrilled to meet her chap and welcome him into our home. I made the family's traditional chocolate cake which he really enjoyed. On their wedding day Belle asked If I would pass the recipe on. Of course, it was real moment between us both, the change of dynamics in our relationship and the knowledge that perhaps we would not see so much of each other, as she started on a new chapter in her life. We sat Belle and I, in the mayor's parlour, with its stunning scenery, gold edged bannisters, and grand oversized portraits on the wall surrounded by heavy draped velvet material. The chaise longue we shared had a William Morris pattern on it and the grand sofa that shared the space was walnut wood and gold. The alcohol had been flowing, so I had a captive audience of bridesmaids and Belle as I prepared the scene with the family story. The young women circled me as I shared that this was a one-time event. They needed to hold onto the words I was about to share that my mother shared with me, as we all know the importance of understanding that the way to man's heart is through his stomach. 'Please' I whispered, 'do not share this recipe, it's yours as a gift. It will allow you all to impress the best with the only moist chocolate cake recipe I know'. The dresses sparkled and the ladies were mesmerised at my words. I reached down to my handbag to reach for the recipe card and then shared with the group the cut out of the front of the box from Betty Crocker Chocolate Fudge cake. There were shrieks of delight and the warning, always finish with an icing sugar top to keep your traditional cake recipe safe and for safe measure, make your own butter cream.

When I look back, I know that God gave me these precious moments with Belle because she was going to play a huge part in our life and in our youngest sons' early formative years. Then of course in supporting him and all of us through a very dark time it is our Father God who is all knowing, which is something I never tire of hearing.

Proverbs 16:9
We can make our plans, but the LORD determines our steps.

7
TSUIN

The chapter title means Twin in Japanese which is appropriate as one summer we were asked to have twin girls despite having registered our room as a single room. The room was plenty big enough for a double bed and so perfectly fine for two singles, but having students was never about the money, it was about bringing the rest of the world in and making the visits count not just for us, but for young people who came. It was not a regular thing either, as often the room was taken with unexpected guests and I never knew how long their stay would be. Some visits were short just a matter of months and others stayed for over a year or longer.

The girls were thirteen years old and incredibly giggly; imagine the highest pitched giggles you can and then double it. The girls stayed for three weeks and for most of that time giggled either through embarrassment and not knowing the English to respond to the situations they found themselves in; Or because they were sharing a private joke, due to language barrier. As minors, my daughter or I would take on the role of mentor, walking with them to school, escorting them to various meeting points for trips. Every day the girls were smiling and giggling. The only challenge we faced was getting them up to get them to school, I have never known two girls to sleep so much. I would knock and go in and talk and wave my arms expressively to no avail, the girls remained motionless and asleep. Honestly, no matter what I did, both girls slept through it. The answer, I found by accident, which was to sit in the kitchen and put the bread in the toaster and turn it up to six. Inevitably the smoke alarm would go off terrifying the girls out from the bedroom in blind panic. I would run up and find them outside the bathroom shocked into 'morning mode' but still giggling. I would go into their room and grab a selection of clothes to reinforce that they needed to go to school and not back to bed. On one of these early burnt toast mornings, I had been waiting for over an hour for the girls to come down for breakfast. Usually, after the burnt toast alarm, they were fairly good at getting ready, so I went back up to give them a reminder we needed to leave for school. I found both girls sitting on the landing floor outside the tiny bathroom, giggling and chatting but still undressed. I knocked on the bathroom door thinking one of my own had jumped the queue, but there was no answer. I opened the door. The smell of stale vinegar hit my nostrils and my eyes caught sight of my bath which was completely splattered with a burgundy spray of vomit, no porcelain white to be seen. I went into auto pilot as this could go only be my eldest Alan, after an impromptu night out. I shut the door and signaled 'wait' to the girls and went to Alan's room, praying the vomit was all in the bath and that he had not choked in his sleep.

'Alan! You okay?' he was face down on his mattress, lanky legs sprawled apart and his long blonde locks matted from a sweaty night's sleep, he groaned and mumbled.

'I made it to the bathroom, better than the floor, right?'

'Better not at all' I sang, as I went back to clean the bathroom and get the girls to school.

Did I mention Alan is Tigger? He was either extremely happy, bouncing about the kitchen picking up various seasonings and making an incredibly good Bolognese sauce or he was extremely sad, hiding away for hours, picking at his skin with sharp objects until he scarred. There were two patterns of response to the alcohol Alan consumed, and please don't assume from that statement that he was always drinking. Just see the teen and the emotional baggage that sits with many of them as well as the unmet mental health needs; the alcohol was a form of self-medication. On a good day, he would come home, waking me up as he came in through the hallway. I would call out 'Is that you Al?' and he would invite me down to the kitchen to talk. I would spend hours listening to some mad idea or other. These ideas stretched to complete drawn up plans that he had laid out inside of his head. My role on these early morning conversations was to listen or challenge his creative thinking. On one night, I woke at 2am to the smell of roast. I thought I was having a stroke but of course that is toast! My room is on the ground floor of this Victorian house, and even that may be wrong, not the floor but the era of the house. it could be late Georgian, early Victorian, I am never sure of historical periods. Anyway, when we moved here, I had three children; Alan and Cherrie who were from my marriage to Keith, then Nick and I had Jonathon, later came Gertie Grace and Rupert. As the family grew, we moved rooms until eventually we took the original living room on the ground floor as it was the largest and nobody used it because wherever we were in the house the children followed. Nick and I were always in the basement kitchen or dining room, so were the children. It seemed silly to stay in the smallest room, when the living room was rarely used so we switched. At this time, we all switched rooms and our spare room moved to the first ground floor room. This was the room Belle and I had decorated.

Back to the toast - I mean roast. It was 2am and I was close enough to the kitchen to smell these delightful aromas, but my mind would not accept them as it was 2am! I became more alert as chatter and laughter reached my ears, so I got up and made my way downstairs. I could see Alan over the banisters sitting at the kitchen table with two complete strangers, all three of them huddled round empty plates and bottles of wine.

Alan made introductions and I am only sorry I do not remember their names. It turned out this lovely lady hosted meals in her home and had got chatting to Alan in the bar where he was doing the sound engineering for a local band and invited him along. From the invite Alan received he then spoke about his famous roast dinners and everyone became hungry and so of course he invited them back to eat! I mean why not? When you are Tigger just about everything is a good idea and of course should be done immediately. At the time of course there is a sense of disbelief of what is going on in my kitchen. I could have screamed out 'No Alan this has to stop'! It would not be the first or last time that Alan and I would have a shouting match, but on this occasion the scene in my kitchen played out as it would at the theatre. This obscure 2am roast with two strangers, all three gently chatting, showed that friendships grow from the most unexpected chance meetings and generally people are good. It must be said right here right now that Alan really knew how to put together a roast and there is nothing like a good meal to bring people together, albeit a cheat version of the real thing.

To return to Alan's drinking. On a bad drinking day, he would bang on the front door, slumped on the railings, cold and unable to place his left foot over right. On a bad alcohol day, I would get him upstairs with Nick and lay him on his front with his head slightly over the mattress aiming towards the bucket. I would check his pockets and often find lavender blossom in them; you were not expecting that were you? We love lavender and my mother, Alan's Grandma, taught most of the grandchildren to run their hand through over-hanging lavender plants. Grabbing the flower as you did so, so the blossom could be rubbed between your palms and you then place your cupped hands over your nostrils and breathe in the calming scent. As Alan got older, he usually carried a tiny pair of scissors and would trim these over hanging plants, bringing the stems home to be placed into a pint glass or egg cup dependent on length of stem and place this on his bedside table.

It is incredible to think that despite the splattered bath moment, the girls had a lovely time with us and reported that they enjoyed the family they stayed with. Then the day came, time to go home. The girls were well known for lateness and so much time was spent informing them of the morning routine. A whole week's notice was given in preparation for the taxi to the airport. The school's translator was called in also, to discuss the plan for travelling home and reassured me that the girls would be ready. Of course, on the day they were not ready, the airport taxi arrived, its diesel engine rattling at 5am on the road outside our house with our neighbour's curtain twitching. I hurriedly went upstairs to get the girls and saw to my dismay that all their clothes were strewn all over the floor.

'Time to go' I called, 'time to go, up, up, up!' I called and clapped my hands together. Nothing, there were just sleeping teens. I started to stuff their clothes into bags and collect their gifts together.

Suddenly the girls were wide awake wanting me to leave their things alone. So, I left the room and went to speak with the airport taxi driver and hoped he would wait a further few minutes. When the girls appeared, I left them putting their cases in the car and ran upstairs to check the room. When I went in, I saw that most of their things were still on the floor, however the suitcase under the bed which had Gertie-Grace's toys in was empty. No, surely not! I wondered and ran downstairs to catch the airport taxi. As we pulled out the cases and opened them up there were all Gertie-Grace toys including her set of Angelina Ballerina. Why? It was never clear, but such a relief to know I had the foresight to check the room. What on earth can you get from that I am unsure, for us as a family, we never placed high value on things. Yes, we have things and the children had a choice of gifts they placed on the Christmas list, however they did not have pocket money and never asked for things daily. The very fact that the girls thought it was okay to take away the toys that belong to the little girl of the family is very strange, but it brings to mind those possessions do not make us happy or content.

I have been blessed through reflection and spiritual growth to have no need any longer for shops and their sales. I used to place so much of my time in searching for bargains, giving the gifts that spoke of the love I felt. It wasn't that I was not a Christian, it was that I had not received enough of His daily bread, His word, gained the understanding I needed to what was expected of me as a Christian. After all Christ died for me, He died for you. This act was out of total unconditional love and the forgiveness of sin, past, present, and future. Had there been a contract it would have said, try, try hard to follow the commandments, strive to be better, follow Me. Be a fool for Christ and nothing else. I was a fool for shopping, it had become therapy for me, as it is for so many. Now I am just a fool for Christ; I heard on Christian radio the question being asked..." who are you a fool for?"

Philippians 4 12-13

I know how to live on almost nothing or with everything. I have learned the secret of living in every situation, whether it is with a full stomach or empty, with plenty or little. For I can do everything through Christ, who gives me strength.

How is your faith?
Journal here!

†

8
ANA

The age of the students I hosted changed with every birthday of the children; Alan and Cherrie were now young adults and we were hosting teachers and mentors, anyone 18 and over.

This relinquished the need to escort students to school, plus drop off and pick up from trips, but mainly it took away Burnt Toast mornings. This summer the School of English was updating their administration systems, so we were asked once again to fill in the family profile. I always felt a little embarrassed when writing down our love of animals, our two dogs and copious number of cats, all rescued at the time. Then I would add the children and would always need extra paper. Fortunately, I did not need a family profile to know how complicated our family dynamics were. What I knew was, that we had someone arriving at 8pm. We had received no profile so did not know anything about the person arriving.

I remember Alan was finishing a B tech at college in computing, everything he knew was self-taught.

He vowed the course had taught him nothing, but he liked his tutor, so hung out there. The fact is, he passed with distinctions and I am sure improved on the knowledge he had already built up.

Immediately after leaving college he came home late one afternoon and told me he had got a job at Canterbury Cathedral. The story he wove was that he had been sitting outside the Cathedral drinking coffee and accidentally had got through their firewall, so he knocked on the

Cathedral office door and explained what had happened. Adding to his explanation, he told them what they needed to do to fix it. At this moment I must add that Alan is autistic and so his perception of a given situation will be 'off center' to the events that happened. It's not a lie, it is simply just how an autistic person sees things. Which is why when discussing autism symptoms, people will refer to autistic people being fixed on a matter or a situation like a dog with a bone. I often think it is no different from colour blindness. A person who cannot tell red from green will always see red differently and it will be a challenge to explain what it is they are seeing, especially as we cannot get inside their head and know truly how a person with colour blindness sees the colours they see. Alan's tale of the events that led to his job will not be accurate, if at all, but I was incredibly proud. My bouncy Tigger with all that entails was working and sharing with me the pitfalls and benefits of updating your computer system.

Ana turned out to be our new guest and took us all by surprise by arriving at 5pm. No sooner had we shown her the house, walked past five cats, stopped the dogs from barking and introduced her to the children, she burst into floods of tears. It turned out Ana had not received our profile either. Ana had requested to stay with adults only, no pets and 'definitely' no children.

'See' said Alan, 'pitfalls.'

This poor lady was devastated, her first-time teaching in England and she got me! I telephoned the school's out of hours service, but it was out of hours! The following morning, I showed Ana the way to school and went in to change her living arrangements. Sue or Shirley, maybe Sharon, I can never remember, organised the host families, time tabling everyone to everywhere - she was a master at her craft. Sue needed to move a rather large amount of people to meet Ana's requirements and began to put the wheels in motion. You can imagine my surprise when at dinner time Ana came in and said in defiant tones she was staying. Ana explained that perhaps this was the push she needed to face her fears and anxieties, not exactly what you want to hear that you are someone's fears and anxiety but there it was and here we are I thought.

At dinner we all ate well, this is all we managed to do, and I consider it a success. Ana was so scared of the dogs that she shook through her meal, the rest of us murmured in strong whispers the words 'Sit, Down, no' and 'Wait'. Through a re-visit of dog training, we all managed to eat dinner. Social interaction for the first week of Ana's visit was with dogs and cats, people in that first week were second class citizens. Incredibly by week two Ana was able to sit and eat a meal while ignoring the Dog's; she told me that she was the only child of academic parents. I do not remember what her parents did for living but they were top of their field, leaving Ana with a continuous stream of adults for company. This would make sense then, to preferring adults to children and pets, after all we become familiar and comfortable with what we are exposed to.

Alan was much the same, he had grown witnessing a lot of trauma, passionate arguments and confrontation were normal for him in his early years. Fighting for praise and approval from Keith his dad was normal, so when we clashed his default response was the same as he gave his dad as a child, screams, tears, and trauma. For Ana, life did not involve children or pets and this unknown entity fed her adult fear.

Ana was now in week four and children have a sixth sense of how to behave or what might be expected of them. Rupert, our youngest, used to plonk himself beside Ana, leaving no choice but interaction as an option. Ana not knowing how to interact would reach for a book and by day three of week four, they had both built a reading routine. Gertie-Grace enjoyed fairies and dance, so put on shows for all to watch and again Ana became a captive audience.

The other day I found a little book that I had intended all my students to sign before they left. This never happened, I am scatty and forgetful however, Ana had signed it: 'I arrived not liking children or pets and now I like both, you changed my world'.

This got me thinking that we are all capable of change if we want it, however sustaining the change can be challenging. God offers us that. He changes us from the inside out and we are so much better for it, more loved with a clearer vision and we hope, more Christ-like.

It is a clear message that He gives us - if we ask, He will make the change! Although there is also another picture painted here.

> Matthew 19:14
>
> "But Jesus said, "Let the children come to me. Don't stop them! For the Kingdom of Heaven belongs to those who are like these children.""

Jesus loves children. He told us that we needed to accept the Kingdom of God like a child, so trusting is their belief. My children in their innocence, did not pick up on Anas' fears and so were unable to place judgement or question her behaviour and just accepted her as she was. This is what we need to remember to do. Love one another without judgement, without prejudice, just as they are, as we are loved by Jesus in this way. It is an amazing love that we should be sharing with others every minute of every day. The trouble with loving our neighbour as our self, is that we don't. We are only human, and our human nature pushes at the Godly nature and before we can squash our human responses, they are out there, judging, gossiping, responding, and leaving our Father ashamed. At that moment in our life we are not showing Christ's love for us, we are not the disciple we should be, yet still He forgives us and loves us unconditionally.

How does God's love feel to you?
Journal here!

✝

9
NABOB

Nabob means a person of conspicuous wealth and or importance, it seemed the only appropriate name to fit the story as the chapter will reveal. Nabob was one of our youngest students, Nick had gone up to meet him at the school. All we knew was that we had an eleven-year-old to take care off, no other details had been given and Nick waited for the airport bus with everyone else. When the bus arrived all the students were assigned a family except Nick, who was told to go home and wait for Nabob who was going to be dropped off separately.

When Nick arrived home, he called out and I went upstairs with a tray to offer a drink of milk and cookies. There was Nabob, a well-dressed young man who looked younger than eleven, I would have given him a generous nine years of age. We showed him to the room, the one Belle had decorated.

Nabob looked around and smiled. I straightened the bedspread and asked if he wanted to come downstairs, he did not. He seemed to indicate that I might like to unpack his bags and I thought why not unpack his bags? My children I know would feel incredibly awkward in this situation, as did I, because Nabob had little English and was far from home. I unpacked and chatted quietly not knowing if he was following my conversation. I turned to see him pull down the quilt and took that as a hint to leave him to settle for the night. As I left the room, I could hear he had turned on the television and felt a little better that he was okay enough to be curious about British TV.

When I arrived in the kitchen Nick was hopping from 'foot to foot' bubbling with conversation. He was telling Cherrie that Nabob had arrived in a limo, not just a limo but with a bodyguard, a huge bodyguard who was carrying a gun! I was not sure what I felt about that, we had never had anyone famous here before; Nick looked and asked 'Why do you think he is famous? He could be Mafia!'

I giggled at the thought of this small built eleven-year-old running a mafia outfit and Nick piped up...

"No, not Nabob, his father maybe?"

Now this really put a different spin on things, and I sat there at the kitchen table thinking about Nabob learning English to take over his father's business. Ridiculous, I told myself, that is an imagination gone wild.

Through the week we took Nabob back and forth to school and was told he could go into town on his own for a couple of hours each day to meet his peers. The town at this time still had shops. The high street was surviving, not brilliantly, as some shop fronts were boarded up, but most were doing well, including Game. One evening Nabob pretty much fell through the front door, the front door was an old brown colour and paint was delicately peeling from the base, so it had a shabby chic look about it. Not that the colour is needed for this story, but I am aware that the front door for each of these chapters was probably a different colour. We live in social housing and the house was regularly painted until now; now there are cutbacks and we paint the door ourselves. As I was saying, Nabob fell through the door and the contents of three extra-large shopping bags spilled out. My Jonathon had come upstairs to see what the commotion was about, and his eyes looked on with envy, for what laid out on the floor was all his birthdays at once. There was an Xbox 360, the latest Halo game, a Halo helmet which my Jonathon had asked for, but we had refused as they were £99.00 and made of plastic. The list did not stop there as there were also two Apple mobile phones. We gathered Nabob's shopping, packed it all into his room and made our way downstairs.

We rang the school to ask if the limit on spending had been removed and what were we to do with this and how was he to get all this back home? These questions and a few more were left on the answer phone as school had now closed. We would have to wait till the morning.

The following morning was the Oxford university trip and so Nabob was away all day. Sue telephoned and explained to me that Nabob's stay was being managed differently to other students and we had a number to call if there was an emergency... 'Did we consider this to be emergency?' she asked. Well of course it was only shopping, it was not an emergency. It may have been a lot of shopping and the amount was more than Nick earned in six months, but still it was not an emergency.

"Mafia, I tell you". Nick was still harping on in a heavy whisper that evening just as Nabob came home. Once again Nabob had a lots of carrier bags, mainly full of Oxford University sweatshirts. I laughed and told Nick perhaps his father was the Kazakhstan version of Del Boy.

The biggest challenge we had that summer was going in to clean after Nabob left, the room was not dirty, and we had bought Nabob two more suitcases to take all his purchases home. The difficulty we had, was the Halo helmet. The model which Nabob had bought, had been dismantled. Obviously because he thought it was a real Halo helmet to wear. Jonathan saw it broken and in pieces and new one Nabob had bought to replace it with in his suitcase. Such extravagance is hard to justify to your children when you budget and live hand to mouth; when you teach them about saving and buying R.U.G.S. RUGs are what my mother encouraged us all to always buy, 'Really useful, gifts'; things you need and things that will help you either in the moment or in the future. Of course, she was right, I always enjoyed the anti-wrinkle cream she bought me, it was a RUG and meant I did not have to pay out for a pot.

On the day Nabob was collected, Jonathan spent several hours trying to rebuild the helmet but in Nabob's eagerness to turn the helmet into a wearable item he had damaged it beyond repair. The limo pulled up outside the library, the driver in a jet-black suit and carrying his broad shoulders, walked towards us as we waited on the step as a family with Nabob. He nodded a silent greeting, effortlessly picked up all the bags. Then Nabob and the driver made their way to the limo. It was almost a Lilo and Stitch moment, one with tingles, for we had shown a moment of ordinary life to this boy. Once the car was out of sight, I looked at Nick and mouthed the word Mafia, then Jonathon piped up, 'Did you see the gun'?

Money always causes a problem whether you have it or whether you don't. Jesus tells us we need to give up our earthly possessions to follow Him. I marvel at the disciples, who dropped their fishing nets and followed Jesus. I imagine they had wives and family and yet they just dropped everything on the spot and followed Jesus. They saw what many did not, He is the Son of God. Their daily work and earnings meant nothing to them compared to the love they felt for Jesus. That is what we need to do, ensure we are giving up what we do not need for a better relationship with Jesus. We should not choose to be controlled by what sits on the shop's shelf or pops up as an ad on our phone. When we become so fixed on what each person has and the need to have it too, we do not open our eyes to the world in front of us. We do not see the homeless chap begging for food, or the elderly lady who is hoping you will say hello. We fail to see our Father in everything we do because we are so fixed on what we want and what we think we need, when in fact all we need is Jesus. This fixation is human nature, it is in us all and can be a huge challenge to step away from. I honestly believe that when we do step away from our addictions, the veil is lifted. We see more clearly the person in front of us, not just the moment but we see their open heart, their story, their hurt and perhaps hopelessness. We see the joy and faith in the cross of those we worship with. When we truly follow Christ, we truly gain our vision.

John 3:17

" If someone has enough money to live well and sees a brother or sister in need but shows no compassion—how can God's love be in that person?"

Matthew 19:21-22

Jesus told him, "If you want to be perfect, go and sell all your possessions and give the money to the poor, and you will have treasure in heaven. Then come, follow me. "But when the young man heard this, he went away sad, for he had many possessions.'

In Matthew 19 we learn that to have eternal life we need to give up our possessions and give to those more in need. An analogy would be to have latest I phone and be told; give that to that chap over there who has nothing. Now I know 'I phones' are extremely expensive but I am also thinking about how we all rely heavily on our phones; we panic when we cannot find them and feel a sense of loss when we lose the information on our phones. To be told to give your phone and all that it holds on it, to a complete stranger is a big ask.

The man Jesus spoke to could not see the danger he was in, he loved what he had, I do not doubt he recognised Jesus, but he loved his possessions and status more. We need to look at our heart and know if we are living our life for Jesus or our own gratification.

Think for a moment, what if Jesus came up to you today and asked you to give up everything and follow only him, would you?

John 3:17

"If someone has enough money to live well and sees a brother or sister[a] in need but shows no compassion—how can God's love be in that person?"

How have you been in a situation like this? Journal here!

10
MARA

The meaning of Mara is bitter and that is not necessarily a negative, as bitter herbs can change a meal to something beautiful, it can be a complimenting trait to one's character.

Mara and I had a deep connection from birth. It was one of those moments where your parents bring you together and then use that opportunity to share birthdays, to ease pressure at family events by inviting the other along, leaving no choice but for a relationship to grow. Remember though, that relationships can be beneficial or disastrous. They hold twist and turns and are ever changing, like a winding, ancient Yorkshire stream. This was my relationship with Mara, for the first half of my life it was interdependent and the second half of my life we became estranged.

So, it is no surprise then that when Mara asked for help and needed a place to stay, I offered. After all, despite differences a person in need is a person in need and we should, if our eyes are open, help those who are vulnerable. This vulnerability is often born out of circumstance and can impact on anyone at any time, through breakdown of marriage, homelessness, disability, redundancy, ill health, anxiety, depression and so the list goes on. Mara ticked four of those on that list and at this stage in the timeline we were doing okay, although you could see we were heading towards a breakdown.

Our priorities had changed, and we had nothing in common anymore. Mara had always needed admiration and attention to get along. She had lived with continuous criticism from her parents, this may not have been the case, but it was certainly her perception. Remember the colour-blind scenario I mentioned earlier, red is blue. Mara is there, her childhood was extremely difficult, despite others relating a more realistic account.

Mara also struggled to see her own participation in the events of her timeline, refusing to take responsibility. I am not saying that we are all to blame for the events we come across in our lives, but we must be accountable for the part we played in those events, after all the Lord allows us to make choices. It is only by looking at situations clearly that we can move forward healthily and leave the bad and hurtful moments in the past, otherwise we risk turning into pillars of salt which is no good for anyone. True forgiveness comes only when we can forgive ourselves and forgive others. I learned recently that forgiveness is when we can hold no resentment for the hurt caused by others, that we let go. We are owed nothing, it equates in the bible to cancelling a debt, and Jesus tells us this.

> It is also clearly mentioned in Corinthians 13:4-5 "Love is patient love is kind....it keeps no account of Injury."

This means we must move forward, we forgive, and that forgiveness is seen in our behaviour, as true forgiveness is a clean slate. So, take that person who you are reluctant to say good morning to, well you need to say good morning. That church goer who says they stand in Christ alone but is distant from you because of all the hurt you have or have not caused. Unless they truly forgive as the Lord tells them to, they are not truly standing with Christ. Having said that I genuinely believe we remain a work in progress for the Lord, He loves us regardless and He wants all of us to love others, regardless. Only God knows our heart, and He is all seeing and all knowing. Mara was recovering from a messy break-up and was now dating a person at her works. The break- up had cost her dearly in that she lost, for a time, her relationship with her daughter. Mara had been living with this chap she was dating from work. Frustrated they had got onto a rocky road, not really having known each other long, she decided she needed to move. In her haste to move in with this chap of hers, she had given up her tenancy and was now homeless. So, when she asked to stay, of course I said, 'Yes stay.'

Mara had this crazy, wonderful, beautiful ability to organise dirt. I mean literally, her garden sat up so tidily it was as if she had weighed and sifted every inch of soil, prior to placing it around the

plants. Some people are just incredibly good at taking chaos and turning it into art. When we got the go ahead to move here, I immediately spoke to Mara to get support. Insanely, after supporting my other nine moves, she still said yes and arrived equipped on the day. We had a huge amount of stuff, I did not throw toys away, as they are so expensive. Jonathon, a baby had his own things, Alans' things and had inherited Cherries' toys as well. The home we left had a double garage which we had filled.

There was no garage in the home we were moving to and no loft. It really was going to be a mission and with so much to sort out, Mara was the person to get on board.

When the day of the move arrived, it was a long tough day, but at the end of it, Mara had unpacked the kitchen, ensured we all had beds to get into and a hot meal to eat. I know! If that skill could be bottled and the essence allowed to drift and seep into us at such moments as these, we would be a nation of Brits with well organised cupboards and no hoarding hidden in the nooks and crannies. Boot fairs would become a thing of the past, because if something new came in then the something old would leave.

On Mara's moving in day the black sacks and boxes of books were too many to count. I was concerned for the little spare room and how Mara would cope feeling so squashed in. I need not have worried, as when I popped up with tea, I did not recognise the room. Gone was the guest room feel of just a few items here and there. Instead, the books were piled up to the ceiling in neat pillars and around the bed, this gave the look of a quirky four poster. Cushions adorned the bed and darker curtains were up on the window. The small balcony door was open, and I spied a wooden trough filled with small fresh green plants. It really looked quaint, as if Mara were selling a lifestyle in a magazine article.

It was heart breaking to see how deflated Mara had become, she was not feeling as if she had any life. Each morning I would a get call and she would be in tears over this chap she had not known that long. With hindsight, I can see all the hurt she felt for this very new relationship was re-triggered trauma for the thirty-year marriage she had not grieved for.

I gathered through her tears how cross she was with my previous advice, which was to not sign up to a loan with him. It was this advice which had added doubt to the commitment of the relationship. The tears were daily and nightly; texts arrived, and I tried my best to give informed advice to support Mara in making an informed decision. Forgetting myself, how difficult it is to see the woods from the trees when we are shattered into a thousand pieces. Offering good advice that is based on fact only can be difficult to hear, due to the many years we had known each other, I knew all of Mara's flaws, just as she knew mine. I do not come out clean in this, but every story has its protagonist and the supporting character. The best advice was of course to wait, what is the rush? There had already been a few boyfriends all ending in tears, there had also been a previous chap who had moved into hers. The question was asked again - what was the hurry? Why the rush? The opportunity had been given to spend time with her youngest daughter. Mara's answer to bonding with children and taking a break, was that her children will always be around, but this opportunity may not. I moved the conversation onto prenup agreements, this conversation topic was not mine but Tom's. Tom is my stepfather and he was equally fond of Mara. He felt strongly that she should not rush where angels feared to tread but be armed and protected. The prenup idea was shouted down. We discussed building friendships, spending more time with this chap before changing so much of yourself. Sadly though, as the words left my mouth, I knew we had reached the end of our path. Our ideas and values had completely changed, and it is a challenge to maintain a friendship that is based on such contrasts of opinions.

Only six days after moving in, I had come home early to ease a severe migraine, when I heard thumping around at the top of the house - was Mara home? I texted but got no response. Then the front door opened, banged and opened again and more thudding. Clearly Mara was moving out and was not wanting to share the next step in her life with anyone. Another bang of the door and more thumping that must be the books, I thought. I really could not be doing with the drama, I guessed she was moving back to the chap and that was fine, she was on her journey after all. What irked was the need to sneak about as if I was a parent not a friend, the need to sneak summed up the history of our relationship; I was always the one who advised and gave the listening ear, taking on the parent role. Dynamics were now changing and there was a need to move forward not back. I laid on the sofa listened to the boxes scraping on the floor until the door banged shut for the last time.

There is a lifetime of goodness that I occasionally search for when I reflect on my time with Mara. But I am human and take far more from the trauma I was left with, than remembering the past we celebrated so much. We all do it, remembering the worst of times more than the best of times.

I am pleased to say that now I reflect periodically on the good, because to have Christ in me means just that, I have Christ in me. My human nature half will gnaw at the bone and continue to chew it over, this is unhealthy and creates bitterness.

I came to Mark 6:11 when Mara left.

> "...and if a place will not welcome you or listen to you, leave that place and shake the dust from your feet as a testimony against them.'

I felt that the time had come to wipe the dust from my feet and walk away; I feel that this reflection had also come to Mara's mind. It was incredibly sad but to quote my dear mother in law, 'it is what it is.' We were done and there was no more that we could do. Just as God can place people in our lives to help them or for them to help us, He can also remove them, prune out the bad and move forward on a different path. I read on social media, written by an incredible man Nick Vujicic;

"Every time you think you are being rejected, God's actually redirecting you to something better. Ask Him to give you strength to go forward".

What are you praying about?
Journal here!

†

11
RUTH

Ruth is one of my Goddaughters, named because of Ruth from the bible who was so loyal to her mother-in-law.

As a small baby Ruth would wear these little bows, like a crown, that somehow seemed to grow and change daily, like flowers in vases lined up in a florist shop. These little nuisances amazed me, such a nightmare to keep on and it took real skill not to lose them. I was especially fond of Ruth, her deep blue eyes and biddable personality made her a delight to care for. This was a good thing, as Ruth and I were destined to be together for a long time. Ruth began to stay when her Grandma was unable to have her full time. Her mother, Mara was at university finishing her studies to become a therapist and needed childcare. I was asked and of course said yes, after all, I was unable to work with Jonathon still under a year old and so poorly. It would only enhance my day sharing it with Ruth. Some toddlers have read the manual and Ruth was one of these children, napping when asked to, tidying up and always helping with Jonathon. When he cried his Painful cry, which ripped right through your ears and tore the soul apart, she would place her fingers against his cheek and soothe him. It rarely helped, pain is pain, but she always offered empathy even as a small child.

In the early playgroup days Ruth went missing, not that the staff knew that. I had fortunately arrived at school early, hoping the pram ride would rock Jonathon off to sleep. I crossed the playground weaving the pram and myself across the brightly coloured numbered snake painted on the tarmac and made my way towards the hut which was set back from the main playground. The hut had a small fence around it with a gate, but the gate was never hooked shut. As I walked towards the hut, I spied Ruth walking her little fingers on the fence post in an imaginary game. I looked for the rest of the group, but no one could be seen. It then dawned on me that she had not been taken in after the lunch play! I scooped her up and knocked on the hut door. They nursery staff saw Ruth first, positioned on my hip with her arms holding on around my neck. Her key worker went suitably white with shock as they hurriedly pulled open the door and ushered us in. Ruth clung onto me, although you could not gauge from Ruth why she had not gone in, the question remained as to why staff had not had counted. Ruth did not say a lot, she was noticeably quiet but all smiles as she played with Jonathon while I wrote my complaint there and then.

That is how we rolled Ruth and I, smoothly and always together. Mara was now qualified and working, so any events that went on at Ruth's school were generally happening when Mara was at work. So like every working parent, Mara missed most of these events. Ruth's father would also be at work but came to key events such as Christmas and assemblies. We settled to full time childcare routine during term time which is a lot of time to spend together and we became awfully close. As Ruth reached secondary school our time lessened, but only temporarily as we now entered crisis point for Mara, which was heart-breaking for the whole family. Everything had become disjointed and the family became disconnected, so Ruth moved in. At least this way I was able to have her close and keep her safe and provide the continuity she needed. This period of crisis was like any crisis that you have experienced. Any crisis: it is personal to you and only you. Those close to you are the only ones who can begin to imagine how you are reeling under a mountain of emotions, along with the fear that nothing will be the same again.

It is important to know that Ruth was resilient and driven with raw determination, this characteristic she displayed became Ruth's saving grace as her mother fell from hurdle to hurdle. I watched Ruth burying herself in her studies and in supporting me. You see I am often confused with moments of madness and plenty of 'scatty'. Life took me by surprise every day and despite getting older I still felt that I was fighting puberty! Often, I would fall from one family event to the next.

Ruth organised me, she knew exactly how to get me to follow a timetable and to be more productive and was ably assisted by my hubby Nick. This delightful, strong, beautiful young lady earned her Nickname Pa aka, personal assistant. Ruth was adept at ensuring I was always where I needed to be, which was a wonderful skill she shared with her mother and it made a huge difference to us. After all we were looking after seven children, if we include Patience who was calling every day. Again, no different from other parents, supporting my father-in-law who looked after my mother-in-law who suffered with dementia and my stepfather with early onset Alzheimer's. Life was crazy and soon that crazy would take us all down a very dark rabbit hole.

God is all knowing and although it is only in hindsight that I look back and see that He was with me all the time; however dark it gets, God never leaves despite dark times, the times when we feel so empty and cold and wonder what life is all about, and what is the point of it anyway? In the middle of the biggest storms when we can see no way out, when we are in the middle of the ocean, drowning, that is when we can define a whole new lower level; at that point always remember;

> Isaiah 41:10
>
> "Don't be afraid, for I am with you. Don't be discouraged, for I am your God.
>
> I will strengthen you and help you. I will hold you up with my victorious right hand."

I cared for Ruth until she left for university. Her 6th form years were spent living with my daughter which I am sure helped Ruth prepare for the new adventure. For her 18th birthday, I was able to buy some useful academic books to support her choice of medical study. This birthday was to be the last that we would spend together, and I felt that it was poignant that she was moving to the next stage of her life. I had co-parented Ruth and it was a true honour to be a part of her life, to be trusted to play a part in her informative years. I will always miss Ruth; however, we all travel our stages of life at different times. I imagine millions of miniature railway stations, like in a model village. Each one of us visiting another destination but never catching up. I can reach my hand to Ruth, but she is not there to reach out to mine. Our stories were shared, and we were both ripped apart by trauma, and I am sorry that I was blind to hers as I fell through mine. For it is now as I write and reflect that the bile rises in my throat. I feel sick, numb and my skin still reacts with goose bumps as fear overrides my ability to reach my frontal cortex and make a sensible response, which for me would be to pray. For not long after Ruth, life would change, I refer to the change as The Rabbit Hole, as it sucks you in and in cases like ours, there were either people on the outer rim pushing and the rest, whoever were left, were falling.

Down and down we all would spiral, totally out of control, alone and in the darkness.

12
JEJUNE

The name in this chapter means undemanding, the main message here, is to get across the personality of Jejune who was struggling in university lodgings. A slim slip of a girl who reminded me of a sloth, beautiful eyes and slow to motivate. The house share she had in Halls was challenging and she was experiencing bullying. Despite efforts from student support and the university's housing department, the intimidation had not stopped. It is always heart-breaking for me when I am aware of a bullying problem. I have had first-hand experience of some vicious attacks in school. I stammered throughout secondary, hated my dumpy round frame and because my mother wanted us to speak properly, I was unceasingly bullied for being 'posh', for having a stammer and generally for being a human being.

My mother told me, history has a habit of repeating itself and throughout my school years I struggled and fell, through misunderstandings, bullying, physical injuries, and an inability to retain what it was I was learning. I later learnt that my mother also experienced bullying. She told amazing stories and could keep the class quiet with her animated telling of the Dagenham Store. Long before Old Bear stories, my Mother created a world of shop shelves and toys that came to life. Each toy held a story that reflected the pains of growing up and then each toy would go on a journey and find hope and beneath the childlike style was the clear message that through Christ we can recover. "Always respond with love and kindness," was Big Bear's motto at the end of the story.

Then the pattern re-appeared, this time for my daughter Gertie-Grace. No matter the school, the support, the peers surrounding her, she became the constant target of bullying. At one-point Gertie- Grace was pushed down half a dozen concrete stairs, another time bombarded by bricks as she walked home from secondary. The first significant event was in primary and by a young boy who drip fed poisonous words to her daily: 'When you get home your mum will be dead!' and other chilling sentences. What made these accounts worse was the school's lack of motivation to deal with them. It was not long before my eight-year-old was spun around by her coat only to fall and break her ankle. Still no response from the school in dealing with the matter. What was more concerning is of course that often, a person who delivers the bullying needs as much if not more support, as such behaviour is often a result of trauma.

Back to Jejune who had nowhere to stay. In line with events, this was before Ruth left home and Mara gave up the tenancy for 'the chap'. Of course, I would help; I mean bless Nick, really oh Lord bless Nick! My husband for many of these unannounced house guests would take Martha, our brown 1982 VW camper van and collect various people and their belongings from wherever they happened to be and move them in. He collected Belle from Wales and Cherrie from Bristol. It goes without saying there was an unwritten contract that if Nick moved you in, he would also move you out. On each occasion, Martha's sliding camper door with its heavy satisfying clunk as you closed it, would be filled with belongings and the person taken to the next step of their journey. I am unsure if Martha was used to pick up Jejune or the purple VW that belonged to my neighbour; either way at this point, Jejune moved from Halls and spent time with the neighbour and then moved into our home. Sharing your space with someone is a challenge, even when it is with your own children. There are still differences to sort out and times when you need to find your own space. This is managed by everyone having their own room, which is why we lost the living room. It seemed more beneficial to squish up in the once named dining room, so everyone had their own personal space to live in. We were experts at squishing up in our 16ft by 18ft room living room. On a Saturday, not any Saturday but a Doctor Who Saturday, there would be Alan, Cherrie, Jonathon, Gertie-Grace, Rupert, Alan's best mate Ash, Ruth, and my other adopted daughter Stefanie. I say adopted, Stefanie like Patience, needed support and I ensured I continued to keep an eye on her. Of course, also squishing were Nick and myself, two dogs and various cats. We would share fish n chip Saturday and New Who, balanced on arms of sofas, laying on the floor and myself with my knees hunched up on the sofa to make more room. I was not holding my knees up to hide from scary monsters!

With the house and it's layout, Jejune kind of blended in the walls, undemanding and unnoticeable with her head in the books! She really was the first half of Bjork song 'oh so quiet' released 1995. I had known Jejune most her life and was still waiting for the second half of that song to happen, the bounce and joy of just living. There was no motivation, no oomph, no gumption, no chit-chat, or absurdities. Jejune I am sure is a late bloomer, the one to surprise all. The David to Goliath, Jack and the Giant, the under study to the lead role. Although now, there was nothing until the fridge opened and she got out the cheese! Then the second half of the song chorused out; 'zing boom, wow bam!' Her love of cheese was equal to that of a smoking addiction. Jejune would consume half pound blocks as a snack. Grated or sliced piles looked like mountains on her plate, placed liked art and consumed as if in short supply or rationed. I would watch glued to my own in-house reality TV. It was incredible how much this boyish slim woman could consume, without gaining an ounce on her hips. I wondered about her heart, the fat, her digestion, the cost of my shopping and at the sheer pleasure Jejune got from cheese. This is the only significant thing I remember, that and my mother sending Grandpa down with blocks of replacement cheese. He would have a small freezer bag on his shoulder and stand on the doorstep and say, 'I am not stopping'. He would then snap open the bag, pull out a block of cheese often wrapped in foil, to keep it chilled. It was so funny, it looked as if this elderly grey-haired man, was a drug runner! I would take the foil covered parcel and he would snap shut the bag and call out 'I won't have another one till Saturday, try make it last!' - again very suspicious if you did not know about my house guest. I very much want to add a laughing emoji here, as it really all seemed very odd. Yet this addiction for hardened milk clearly provided comfort. It is not any different from the child having a tantrum to release a difficult day, an adult with a glass of wine after a long day at work, the cigarettes at every coffee break or perhaps the more positive addictions: the daily work out at the gym, the morning run along the prom, the daily yoga spot and the offering of prayer. I have a lot of time for prayer, I am sure the Archbishop of Canterbury once said that when they prayed something happens and when they do not nothing changes, so they keep praying. It may have been as an answer to the question does prayer work? Yes, prayer works, of course we never usually get the direct answer we want but we always get what we need; prayer is like the Rolling Stone song, 'Cant always get what you want, but if you try sometime, you get what you need', So, try sometime. I am sure our church leader told me that God answers prayer with yes, no and maybe later.

This may have come from Alpha. Not that it matters where it comes from, I feel that those words can only add discernment to our spiritual growth.

I don't remember how Jejune came to leave, as with her name it would have just happened in an uninteresting way, the event did not stick, I was able as I had before, to provide support at a moment of need. It was not easy, some who ended staying here were not easy at the time; but it is not for us to judge who is worthy of the support and whether some support should be of better quality than other support. Jesus does not weigh up individual effort to measure the amount of love He will give. Each one of us is as important to Him, as the next person. No matter what we have done, if we repent, surrender our lives to Him and read scripture to help us follow His word. All these things allow the Holy Spirit to get to work which leads us to changing from the inside out, no longer moving towards sin but away and trying to be more Christ like each day. The latter is the toughest challenge as we cannot adapt His word to suit our need; forgive means to forgive everyone, love means to love everyone. We cannot say to one person I will only see you this much because I do not like how you talk to me or behave towards me. We need to love each person the same unconditionally and I challenge anyone to say that this is easy. It is not. God has never said being a Christian is easy, we must feel the sacrifice and if we do not, then perhaps we have become to use to adapting his word to suit our need.

Ask yourself honestly; Do you feel the sacrifice?

Do you feel the sacrifice?
Journal here!

13
SOLO AND EMI

Alan was living around the corner and called in often with a mate or two tagging along. He would either rustle around the kitchen and cook, bounce about and tell great tales of recent exploits or go from room to room chatting to his siblings. This usually created such excitement that structure and routine did not just fly out of the window but left abruptly. Whilst we all delighted in the bouncy 'Tigger's' arrival, these visits often ended in tears, as if we had lived through the great storm of 1987. To Paraphrase Vicar of Dibley, well it was not a storm, more like a great wind!

On this day Alan introduced me to Solo, a musician who was here to produce or play at an event in Alan's local pub. Not that Alan had a local, I think every pub in town that hosted live bands was his local. Solo was tall with dark hair, his manner was laid back, easy to chat to and pleasant enough. He was just trying, like every man in their early twenties, to make their mark in the world.

As we drank tea Alan stated that Solo needed a room just for the week. Ours was empty and of course it made sense to offer, did it not? I mentally threw daggers at Alan's eyes; I mean how dare he put me on the spot like that. I did not know this man, but when did I know anyone who turned up at the house? - not often. One week, I checked:

"Oh yes," replied Solo, "lots to do, not stopping".

So up he went to the attic room, complete with a rucksack and guitar. Once again, the small balcony became the social hub of the house with Alan and Solo using it as a smoking corner and meeting room, ironing out what they could on the technical music front. In the evenings Solo or Alan would eat late and fill the rooms with aromas and noise and I just prayed for a quick end to the week.

The following Saturday was gig night and Solo came downstairs to introduce me to Emi the singer, who would be here for the weekend. Yes, here in my home, with Solo whom she had just met. Solo was a polite young man so definitely did ask permission, but in a way that you felt the decision had already been made.

Gertie-Grace was fascinated by all these goings on, and happily trotted back and forth with various drink orders from Alan; she also sang along with Emi which was a great confidence boost for her. Emi could sing, sometimes people believe they can sing but the truth is its just singing. It is nice but there is not that beautiful tone that reaches the ear. This young lady had that, a new sound which was lovely to listen to.

So now my room had two guests, I never made a thing of it, these two strangers coming together and sleeping in the double bed. They are adults and not my responsibility. By not making a thing of it meant my younger children did not question it. Of course, a few weeks had now passed, and it was beginning to get difficult with Solo and Emi eating at a much later hour each day. Often, I would come downstairs to a messy cooker, which has always been a struggle for me. Then off course late into the evening there would be music and singing, until it was time to go and perform or record at the studio. The one week had stretched into a blur. The niggles for some would not be problems, but for me, Jonathon's ill health meant that I had paced the floors of our house each night since his birth as he dealt with pain. This loss of sleep continued but in a different format, no longer making my arms ache, as Jonathon would be restless, uncomfortable, and feeling sick. Up every eighty minutes, my heart ached with every night that I did not sleep. It is understandable then that I went to bed early, the house shuts down by 7pm. Once the children were in bed settled with audio books and night lights, I would go and rest in bed, put the radio on and just relax and reflect. I believe that down time is so important, and I know this time has allowed me not to go insane over the years. I still do not sleep well; I have this stuck pattern of sleep behaviour from all those years ago. When with Jonathon, we would pace the floor nightly for more than six years and so it became embedded.

Our two impromptu guests, although lovely and clearly smitten with each other, needed to head home for everyone's sake, especially Gertie-Grace. Gertie-Grace loved to be involved but struggled once she was bought into the circle. Emi had embraced Gertie-Grace and also had borrowed her trilby hat. This hat was Cherrie's and had come to Gertie-Grace through Cherrie sorting out her room. It was the first grown up thing Gertie-Grace had been given and it suited her, but she was not confident enough to wear it. Emi also looked fabulous with the hat on and so wore it every moment she had. Gertie-Grace's beautiful soul did not mind Emi borrowing her hat, although she worried that she might not get it back.

It was time to go, Emi had packed and was leaving with Solo. This young man had a beautiful smile and I hoped that he had found his soul mate, that life with this quirky singer would work out for him. For now, though their journey with us was over and they were moving forward. That evening Nick and I shut down the house, wiped the cooker, changed bed sheets, and both rested in bed early, with the children settled to How to Train Your Dragon audio and Paddington Bear. I breathed a sigh as I let go of the past few weeks, my eyes closed and I was ready, so ready to sleep.

We do not see enough the impact we or others have on us; however short or long we all leave a footprint. I heard from Solo a few years on, just as I had forgotten his stay. His email came when we were falling down the rabbit hole and then I understood the footprint we had left. Just think of how many people were impacted by meeting Jesus, or by seeing Him walk through their town or hearing the stories of the unexplained miracles. God planned this journey, His journey, knowing that each person would hold a story and that account would change the lives of many forever, for Eternity, as thousands upon thousands believed in what they saw, the Father, the Son and the Holy Spirit.

Romans 12:1-2

"And so, dear brothers and sisters, I plead with you to give your bodies to God because of all he has done for you. Let them be a living and holy sacrifice—the kind he will find acceptable. This is truly the way to worship him. Don't copy the behaviour and customs of this world, but let God transform you into a new person by changing the way you think. Then you will learn to know God's will for you, which is good and pleasing and perfect."

14
LITTLE PETE

Little Pete was the nickname and it was that simple, Pete was little. I always struggled with nicknames, as a child they made no sense, then I had children of my own and nicknames seem to be much easier and based on a 'say what you see' method. When Alan was in secondary school, he needed to use a laptop, due to hypermobility and difficulty writing, so school was teaching him to touch type. It is not a surprise then if you use the 'say what you see' method that Alan earned the title, aka nickname, of 'laptop man' throughout his school years. When Cherrie was in school, I was mortified when she referred to her friend as Gay Dean. I remember how cross she was with me, asking me what my problem was! His name was Dean and he was gay, and he was happy enough with the title. Little Pete was not just small for a man but small in general. He was smaller than Cherrie. I know that in life there are smaller people and I know there are also taller people. I can only chat about those who have stayed in my home, been offered love and support, and perhaps reflect on what God gave me through that visit. I am not 'highest', but I know Alan did tease his mate on occasion about his height. He often played the small person song that was on Ally McBeal, but I imagine it must have been played in many places internationally too. Alan did not watch Ally McBeal so I am unclear how he knew the song.

Anyway, little Pete was at the door and as he walked in, he looked and smiled and announced Alan was waiting for him as he had some project or other. This is never good news as when Alan had a project, it meant he was developing something for someone and as money was always involved it meant a deadline was in place. When a deadline needed meeting, Alan would call in little Pete to support him with his project. There are so many young people who understand computer tech, other people have a skill to learn many languages. Alan was a natural when it came to computer tech, it came extremely easy to him, just as breathing did for all of us. Pete also had a solid grasp of tech which is why he was always called on to him support at these times. What 'a project' meant for me was two men stationed at my kitchen table with laptops, wires and mother boards. They would remain at the table till the job was done, no washing, no sleep, just fuel in the shape of bacon sandwiches, take out, lots of tea and in the evening several pints of ale.

The drift of their conversation would seep upstairs to my room in the early hours as the house sat rested from a busy family day. This made it more difficult to sleep, so I would pop downstairs to see both men still working amongst packaging of snacks and cigarette papers. The faint odour of sweaty man hung in the air, for a second their conversation stopped while their fingers hovered over the keyboard. I smiled as it felt surreal, as if everything had been paused, as if Dr. Strange had used his science to fix the scene in the hope that good will win over evil.

'Mum' Alan spoke, breaking my drifting imagination which bought me back to present. I gestured with cups in my hands if they needed tea.

'Now is not the time for tea' said Alan and gestured to the thick dark liquid in his mug.

I reached to pick up the mug to sniff at what they were drinking but there was no need, the rich bitter smell of espresso hit my Nostrils followed by ... 'Is that rum?'

Alan shrugged and Pete picked up his mug and took a gulp then blew air from his mouth. Yes, another whiff of coffee and rum which was enhanced by a good amount of morning breath. Rum may be warming and what was needed, but mouthwash would have been better. I looked on again at the array of stuff on the table and decided in the morning to set up another table in the living room. Breakfast was not going to happen for the rest of the family, unless I find another table, I went back to bed with this thought in mind.

I wandered down at six in the morning to silence, was it possible the project was finished. The table still had its tablecloth of stuff on it but there were no laptops and no Little Pete. I took a calming breath and started to clear some of things away, placing all the tech bits into a mixing bowl. Why a mixing bowl? Well, it's not until your son is screaming all the worst words at you because you hoovered his room and then is sifting through the hoover bag to find some diode or other, that you learn that even the smallest piece of metal is actually a computer part. So do not throw any of it away, do not hoover and if possibly just resist the urge to go into his room at all.

As I finished tidying, I heard footsteps. Alan came out of the living room and told me Pete was still dozing. I poked my head around the door and there he was stretched out on the two-seater sofa. Not many people can find comfort on a two-seater, your limbs get cramped before sleep sets in. I found it rather amusing to see Little Pete out for the count and thrilled that we still had a functional sofa for the morning school rush.

It turns out that the particular project had finished, although there were many other occasions that I would wake up to the smell of coffee, rum and morning breath and find Little Pete on the sofa with Alan plugging away at his laptop. Most of the time when Alan saw Little Pete, it was for help and support. I know this was an interdependent relationship as Alan would also go suddenly to help and support Pete as soon as he was asked. I know also that these two young men fought and fell apart quite often. On these occasions Alan would tell me to leave his name out of it!

Yet no sooner was there a project or drama both men were always about for each other.

Jesus is always there for us, no matter what. Of course, he wants us to manage our lives and make good decisions, but we can only do this by having an interdependent relationship with our Father. It works both ways, we need to read scripture, we need to help those who need help. We need to follow God's word each day, apply His teachings, tell others about His amazing love and forgiveness, and yes, it's the latter word that we really need to listen to. We need to forgive, to move forward, no holding onto grudges, no holding onto judging people. Alan's motto is 'stuff happens', you are born, and you die but it is the stuff in the middle that counts. I am sure that this sensible motto comes from the cult TV show Red Dwarf. Though Alan is right, with or without faith, it is the bit in the middle that counts. We should want to make a mark, leave a legacy, whether a kind word, good actions or huge fundraising efforts, volunteering or simply being aware that our responses to everyone are out of love. We should want to make our actions count and impact on many. Consider leaving only blackness and negativity as a legacy is indeed a dark place to be.

The best way of course to manage the difficult task of being simply kind to everyone, is to ensure we can accept and love ourselves. This is achieved through Jesus Christ, by the forgiveness of sin and the revelation that we are loved just as we are. Again, this is not easy. I have spent all my life in a relationship with God and only this week on Wednesday evening to be precise 24.7.19, in the middle of the highest recorded heat wave have I managed to let go of everything, love myself and fully trust the Lord.

Do you trust the Lord?
Journal here!

15
ASH

Alan met Ash at secondary school. From the very first visit to our home, to do whatever tech thing was going on at the time, Ash was then always invited round. Don't get me wrong, Alan did spend time at Ash's. However, I am unsure whether it is because we are on a more direct pub route or if it was because Alan felt comfortable here, but whatever the reason, this house seemed to be the hub of the action. Ash's quiet methodical approach was a complete contrast to Alan's, it is probably why they got on so well. Both young men had also spent a lot of time together and this firm foundation has formed many friendships in the past and will continue to do so. It is having that trust through time spent together, shared experiences and problems resolved, that forms the best relationship. This is what Alan and Ash were building on currently. It's by no means a surprise then that much of Alan's and Ash's early friendship, post-secondary school, was spent in the pub; then back from the pub to here, to eat, drink some more, discuss life, the universe and everything. Maybe on these occasions they would binge watch some television and of course as time passed Cards against Humanity kicked in and the evening routine had a new game to fill the drunken hours. On these nights Cherrie and Jonathon would come downstairs and join in with Cards against Humanity, as time went on, although probably not old enough, Gertie-Grace would join in. To listen to such gregarious bouts of laughter was a real pleasure, to be honest I still have no clue to the rules of this game. I joined in once with Cherrie and Alan, laughed a lot but have no idea on what went on.

After drunken nights, I would find Ash on the sofa in the morning, he never painted a picture of events, never embellished what went on.

'Good night?' I would ask and Ash would proceed to tell me that yes it was a good night and he was still extremely drunk but threw up on the doorstep and that between him and Alan, they had taken water up to wash the vomit away, so I was not to worry.

There were many nights like that one and many more others spent just watching films and eating. Although Ash never officially lived here, he spent enough time here to qualify as a resident; by year eleven in secondary, he had become my other son. This honorary title was befitting as it was Ash's methodical approach to life, one that balanced Alan's hyper approach, the more so when Alan's bipolar caught hold of him. The super happy moment dissolved as quickly and as violently as salt on a slug, turning to complete despair with no outlook or hope. It was reassuring when these times swamped him, to know that Ash would be there.

A relationship with God with Jesus Christ is not dissimilar to that of a good relationship with your parents or best friend. Ash and Alan were there for each other, the worst times and the best times. There was never any judgement just acceptance and always forgiveness, however difficult. Unfortunately, Alan's bipolar meant there were a few more worst times than most, and it is a bittersweet thing to be thankful that it was Ash who called the ambulance when Alan took an overdose and it was Ash and Sorello who 'talked' him back over the railings that looked over the port. The sweetness of the fall Alan told me was just what he needed at that moment, which is typical for many with autism that they are in the moment only. You are unable to see the next step the outcome becomes inaccessible. It is this thought pattern that leads to the many meltdowns that all parents with an autistic child have experienced. The sheer fear of not knowing what is next, puts anxieties at an extreme level, causing complete panic and the shutdown of the amygdala, which sits at the base of the brain at the back of our necks. When the amygdala shuts down, messages are unable to get to the frontal cortex, therefore the child or adult is unable to reason through any thought process. This process is the same for the traumatised child. I have found over the years that there is a fine line between the symptoms of autism and trauma. Fortunately, at the moments of pain and panic Ash reinforced what it meant to be a friend, he was my and Alan's answer to prayer.

> Proverbs 18:24
>
> "There are "friends" who destroy each other, but a real friend sticks closer than a brother".

†

16
THE RABBIT HOLE

I need to explain how this rabbit hole looks. This is no easy feat, as for each person involved there is a different perspective and another dimension. Let us therefore establish that the hole has so many sides so that neither I, nor anyone else, will never be able to account for all of them. Each side blends with the next, leaving the impression of a smooth circle which indefinitely billows into an immeasurable dark depth. There it sits, the sink hole; sometimes you fall in it and find yourself caught on corners, stuck amongst cobwebs. On other occasions the rabbit hole becomes a permanent object that you automatically step over to avoid, so much so that you no longer see it is there - until you trip and stumble and find your ankle weakens, twists over its side and you are caught out in disbelief. 'How could I forget that it was there?' you ask yourself. You find you are unwillingly falling into its depths again; as you fall, you drift in and out of an almost hypnotic state of over thinking, unreasonable questioning, losing track of time as your daily life ebbs away.

This hole had a beginning, which should have been an significant moment in my life, but the protagonist was unconnected to me and I was off stage being busy with my concerns.

Mara was recruiting friends for her 'soon to be' stepson. A chubby boy, with huge round hazel eyes, but that was it. I struggled to find anything likeable about him, which caused another struggle, as my heart has always been for children. I would chat to this child and listen to his cocky responses and search for something to like about him. He was a small boy who bullied, lied, laughed too loud and shoved his way through primary school. Clearly, he had his own demons to deal with and it was difficult to get along with him. Although it could be said that there was never really a long enough opportunity. Friends are chosen through trust and commitment but he was not someone my two youngest had considered to be-friend, as they had nothing in common with him.

Mara knew this but still insisted on micro-managing, in the hope of fostering a friendship. Unbeknown to me, when Gertie-Grace went off to Judo with her friend Buddy, the step child was there and so was Mara who was gently nudging Buddy and the stepson together. As both the children had registration at Mara's workplace, the unscheduled approach of staff to a child out of work hours was a problem but not a big one. Mara failed to consider these actions and decided to chat to Buddy while Gertie-Grace had gone to the loo. Mara discussed the benefits of a friendship with her stepson, not so bad in the big scheme of things. Then Buddy repeated this to his parents later, that Mara had said that Gertie Grace was not a nice girl and Buddy really should not bother. This made Buddy feel pressured and scared and because this happened out of work hours was rightly considered a safeguarding concern. The whole scenario should not have happened, with a little thought there were a thousand other outcomes that could have been achieved.

I could only wonder at what was at play; for those who have slipped down a slippery slope, you may well testify to a fallen angel, Lucifer maybe. I truly believe in a darkness, in temptation being a great pull on our needs, whether it is greed, addiction, control, hunger or fear. Our own human nature is all the evidence you need, when we consider the lengths people will go to, to get what they want whether it is pay back, revenge, the latest phone, the next fix. Human nature naturally means we have a desperate need to control situations and outcomes. This is an unhealthy road to travel down, a form of darkness that can become the center of our thoughts.

The situation Mara found herself in was due to feeling out of control. She desperately needed to fix her situation, build connections and surround her new relationship with new people. This understanding did not change the confusion Buddy felt when he went home upset and worried and spoke to his parents. This led to Buddy's parents complaining and Mara being invited to chat to her boss. It was not a disciplinary, but it was enough to add humiliation to the rejection she may have felt from the detachment of our relationship. Both feelings re-trigger old hurt and blame and must be placed somewhere. It seemed irrelevant that I had nothing to do with the scene that played out, or the consequences that resulted from her conversations with Buddy and then later with her boss.

Yet still it was there, that human need to control and to look at the picture while standing too close to the canvas. Mara needed to step away instead she telephoned me because she needed someone to blame. My only part in what had happened was my friendship with Buddy's mother, who to be fair had telephoned me to ask if I had a problem with her complaining to Mara's boss. Why would I have a problem? 'You need to do what's right for you,' were my words. I felt confident that Mara was a professional and would not place blame on my doorstep for something that did not involve me. My words echoed in my head, despite not playing a part in her staged visit to Judo. Mara screamed down the phone at me and the first scrape of the spade sliced through the dirt and the rabbit hole began.

'How expletive dare you'! The spade scraped again. 'Expletive, expletive, you, expletive bitch!' another scrape of the spade.

'You are so expletive dead to me!' The corners carried on being cut and the rabbit hole started to take shape. Had it stopped there, who knows, we may all have survived. Instead through social media appeared a hefty one-sided dose of one person's story and the words were written out there for the world to see. They took their own shape and became the truth to those who read it.

I am pleased to say that I am not a part of the social media scene, so stayed out of it, my side of the story was woven as it happened. It was never heard and sadly it was never asked for by the masses. Despite the years of silence, I still caught my breath when Mara and I happened to be in the same place at the same time. Incredibly you could count the moments on one hand, when you consider we live in the same small town, that's quite an achievement. Then out of the blue she asked to meet. I went because Grandpa had said to go and Grandpa is important to me. I went as arranged and met with Mara, even though I felt completely sick inside with waves of uncertainty washing over me.

The whole event was surreal, Cherrie came with me, because I needed the skills she had gained in holding a grudge, plus she wanted to keep me grounded as I had done nothing wrong. Mara bought along Jejune; both of us were armed with our support networks and both of us were drowning, however one of us was pushed and the other had jumped, or so it felt.

The outcome I wanted was to be able to attend weddings and funerals and any event that we were both linked to because of a lifetime of connections, without feeling that neither of us had a right to be there. Unbeknown to me Mara wanted an apology, an admittance of wrong doing, of fault, a scape goat. When all is said and done, we want to blame someone else for our part in life's events rather than understand why we behave as we do and grow in faith by asking God for His help, so we can begin to accept the things we cannot change. If I remember rightly, it was New Year's Day when we met. I had dressed up a little and had used a luxury vanilla body cream. A strange thing to remember but Cherrie had bought it for me as a gift and I remember it well because as I stood at the bar ordering our drinks, a happy drunk told me I looked gorgeous and smelt good enough to eat. I had bought a new handbag with me and Mara had bought a spade!

We met at one of Alan's locals where he was doing the sound engineering for the New Year celebrations. We arrived early as I hoped to sit and watch Alan put the equipment together. It is like a work of art and one that never ceased too surprise me, after all Alan was self-taught yet very quickly had become a master of his craft. I missed it all though because Mara had arrived even earlier. We sat at a table near the band and it was awkward, painful and a mistake. As I have mentioned before, there are far too many sides to a story. I thought it had gone well, we agreed to disagree and initially it was nice. I was pleased to see her face. I had missed her, I sat and heard no words as she spoke, instead I was transported back to hanging out of our bedroom window when were thirteen and fourteen years. We were totally smitten with the 'neighbours' two sons over the road. We would lean out of the window with pop music blaring, in hope that either one of them would look up and notice us. For us to be able to hang out of the window at the given opportunity, it meant we had to stay in the bedroom all day. We would move the large bedroom around and became room designers without knowing it.

I felt a nudge on my knee from Cherrie and tried to focus. Mara had voiced she wanted an apology and I was sorry for the feelings she had and we went our separate ways with me finishing that I hoped to see her at Grumpy's birthday. Later Mara voiced on social media and to Grandpa that it had not gone well; the words were misguided and not a true picture and allowed for no future hope.

Nothing can grow from dead bones unless you allow the Lord to have complete control of your life.

Matthew 19:26

"Jesus looked at them intently and said, "Humanly speaking, it is impossible. But with God everything is possible."

Ezekiel 37:4-6

"Then he said to me, "Speak a prophetic message to these bones and say, 'Dry bones, listen to the word of the LORD! This is what the Sovereign LORD says: Look! I am going to put breath into you and make you live again! I will put flesh and muscles on you and cover you with skin. I will put breath into you, and you will come to life. Then you will know that I am the LORD.'"

Then it came, nine months after that event in the pub, a phone call from a concerned bystander. An allegation had been made against Alan, historical abuse and all the nightmarish words that sit with that. Mara needed somewhere to place blame, a small bird had told me that the rabbit hole was down to my not sorting things out, not apologising.

Whatever the reason, Mara had nearly four years of anger and the match, with those close fanning the flames; anyone who was everyone grabbed a spade!

I sat with Cherrie on the end of my bed, I sat and wept, questioning how we had fallen into this mess, how this woven story was being used. Why were we being told now about an allegation? How were we going to support Alan? Alan will struggle, Alan is low, Alan does not process information well, and Alan is extremely unstable. Please know at this point that I have never said that this allegation was a lie, I have never said that this is a situation that I can sit judge and jury over, I can only report facts and this is where we were at.

Alan needed the best of my help but was unlikely to ask, there was too much information to process, too much to consider and too much at stake. Then Cherrie was crying and I was crying. I remember clearly holding onto her so tightly as we fell into the rabbit hole, falling, we were falling, life had no sense to it and we no longer could see its value, the hole was pulling us down, flooding with our tears. I could hardly breathe, gasping for air as tears and breathing became complicated and no longer a simple task, oh my God oh my God we were drowning.

Nick stayed downstairs, managing life, and Cherrie and I did the only thing we could, we rang the police. The phone call was recorded, I explained my concern through sobs and tears, my son must be due in for questioning, there was this feud and people were so cross that this allegation had appeared with all the other horrific words associated with it. My son is ill, the police knew this, they had been to my mother's grave eighteen months before, when Alan was found there. His body sprawled over the winter-soaked foliage, having taken an overdose. 'Could you please ask the person who questions him, at whatever point that is, to telephone me, please?' I cried, 'he will need a responsible adult with him. I know him and if he is unsupported, he will take his life. He is autistic, he is bipolar, he lives in the now, and he will not be able to process the words, the environment, anything'. I cried and made the request three times in that phone call: that I was to be called when they took my son in for questioning. It was November 2014.

I am unsure how we placed one foot in front of the other after that, each time I did, someone else had found a spade and we fell deeper and deeper, there was no light above us, just the blackness, we had fallen so far I did not know how to get out. I did not mention it too Alan as I was too scared to bring the realisation of the situation forward. Like all of us I needed to have some control, plus it was still hearsay.

Then it was Christmas, Alan bounced in already drunk at about eleven in the morning. He had this amazing gift of a Viking drinking horn, bought for him by his girlfriend. He was a happy drunk, every so often shouting SKULL, a native drinking term perhaps, as he raised the horn and drank some more. I heard him sharing whispers with Gertie-Grace, being amazed by Rupert and pouring an ale for Jonathon. Nick and I wondered if he could maintain the flow and he did. I mean cooking the Christmas meal became a delicate task, as I gently pushed over-hanging hot pans back on the stove, following him around the tiny space; we had to finish all the bits he had started. The ovens were on high because potatoes needed to be crispy and Cherrie just wanted him to leave before Christmas was ruined and the grudge embedded. Cherrie had always been Alan's parent and he hated that she had an answer for everything. He would throw all the insults and Cherrie would gently bat them back, but only Alan could throw such insults, if anybody else did he would put them over a barrel. Only he could insult Cherrie, after all she was his little sister. The silence of the house was strange after Alan left. I had stepped over the rabbit hole all day and not noticed it at all, but we were all just about to be violently pushed in and there would be nobody to get us out.

In January 2015 I got an unexpected message from Cherrie, Patience had got in touch through social media, she was really worried about what she was hearing and could we please, if only for five minutes meet up with her. At this point we had not seen Patience since her baby had be born. I am sure I mentioned that our relationship went from fixed to broken; we had reached a broken era and it was this very moment that bought Patience back into our lives again.

So, we met up. Her daughter was now three and struggling with varying needs and trauma. We were not there for this, although the needs of her daughter drove the relationship forward for a long time after that. Patience had heard from those digging the hole and she felt a sense of foreboding. She was confused as to what this was about but wanted to know if we were all okay. Cherrie explained the only side we had to the hole and we all cried again. This time a cry escaped my lips like that of a wounded animal and I felt bereft.

The hole had been left unseen for about ten weeks, Cherrie was starting a new job and we were all excited to hear about her day. At moments like these, new job, first day and last days, we try and do something special for tea. I cannot remember what Cherrie had chosen as no sooner had she come through the door than her message alert on her phone went crazy. One of Alan's friends was looking for Alan's sister - THUMP - we had been pushed and were now falling down the rabbit the hole!

I could not drive, I shook and choked on vomit that was in my mouth. As we pulled up outside Alan's place there were Blue lights everywhere; we rushed out of the car and across the road and through the open front door to Alan's flat. I stopped, I failed there and then as a mother, I was frozen, frightened and I could not go in. I looked into Cherrie's huge round terrified blue eyes, there were no need for words, a child knows their mother and she raced on ahead of me. It was Monday 23rd March 2015.

Ash was with Alan he had resuscitated him while waiting for an ambulance, they had a heartbeat, then they lost it...then it was faint but there by a thread.

I sat in the car, looking at the blue lights, people crying, strangers whom I did not know who had come out from the flats, people stopping to look as they went past.

'He is breathing' I told Nick, holding the mobile tightly to my ear as if somehow this would bring Nick closer to me. I wanted to hold my babies all so close and never ever let go.

The ambulance crew came out of the building with Alan on a stretcher, the wheels clattered on the steps down from the front door. I could not get a clear view, just a glimpse of his cheap old black comfy trainers. A picture of his tiny new-born feet flashed into my mind. Three ambulance crew were still dealing with him, wires and machines were being held by crew as they raced to the ambulance. Cherrie climbed into the car, her pale face lucid white, the blue lights wailed as I put the car into gear to follow.

The last time I had to follow an ambulance was when my mother collapsed at home. She had had an aneurism and they were still resuscitating her as they raced off with her. All mothers are amazing, my own mother was one of those who had gone the extra mile. My mother had struggled with extremely poor eyesight throughout life, her glasses were thick rimmed and covered her face like science goggles. Then later as fashion changed, she could get away with a pair that looked rather ordinary, until she turned her face and the thick lenses shaping her eye could be seen.

I was fourteen, life was hard, my parents fought like crazy. There was always something to argue about. I was okay though, as whilst I fought with my brother, my eldest sister had been given the parent role at a young age. We had been bought up in the seventies and it was considered perfectly normal to raise a nation of latch key kids, we were part of that community. Both our parents worked so the street kept an eye on all the children. While the street kept an eye on the children that belonged to their council estate, my big sister kept an eye on the three of us. My mother had four children under the age of five and Mary who was the eldest, was not actually that much bigger than me, the youngest. My brother Saul was next, but we did not get along. This was no exaggeration; we were fire and petrol. It was not until Saul had a motor bike accident around my 18th birthday that we clicked, we finally understood each other. It was then I became connected to my brother and it was to be a lasting bonded relationship.

We all went to Sunday school at our local church, which was a full church. It was a time that built resilience, I think. What we learned by going to church was that there was a community to turn to when you needed support. We grew up knowing it was normal to talk about things and okay to share when you were sad. Church was a trusting place to be, it provided fun and games when our parents could not. It provided Barn Dances and jumble sales that brought families together where we all could donate a few pennies to buy our neighbours' toys and take a different bunch of stuff home to occupy the long winter nights. Church forges bonds and a place for mental health to regain its balance. Today children are occupied by tablets and mobile phones, so their parents can have a lie-in. Many children are out of touch with society, unaware of the community they live in, because of this they do not have the skills to share a conversation and are anxious and uncomfortable. There is no network for them to build upon and adulthood, without a network, will only further deskill them.

Our current pandemic may have been a blessing. While anxious children get to remain indoors legitimately, the world of tech has given us online accessible schooling and access to a network of people that for some was nonexistent, unless they were on YouTube. What sits in the forefront of my mind is that when my mother courageously fought breast cancer, her diagnosis prepared me for her loss. However, the aneurism she died from did not and the loss of the matriarch left a chasm between four children. Some people will say that they do not believe in God, yet at a time of crisis they will cry out to the Lord, they will find themselves accepting the offer of prayer. I find celebrating God and thanking Him an easy thing to do, having a heart for gratitude is an easy thing to do. It is much harder for me to cry out to Him. To know a loving a Father and then to know pain, to know that He tells me there is a time for all things. God does not want anyone to feel pain or be hurt. Incredibly I am a testimony that beauty can come from ashes, yet despite knowing a loving Father, I also knew I was heading for a period of severe pain that would raise more questions than it could answer.

I recalled this bible verse, which a band called the Bryds turned into a song in the 1960's called Turn.

For everything in life there is a season, people and drama come and go and it can hurt when you are in the moment. With God in our lives that pain and suffering can be turned into something beautiful, it can be used but of course it all happens in our Fathers time.

A Time for Everything Ecclesiastes 3:1-17

> For everything there is a season,
> A time for every activity under heaven.
> A time to be born and a time to die.
> A time to plant and a time to harvest.
> A time to kill and a time to heal.
> A ime to tear down and a time to build up.
> A time to cry and a time to laugh.
> A time to grieve and a time to dance.
> A time to scatter stones and a time to gather stones.
> A time to embrace and a time to turn away.

A time to search and a time to quit searching.
A time to keep and a time to throw away.
A time to tear and a time to mend.
A time to be quiet and a time to speak.
A time to love and a time to hate.
A time for war and a time for peace.

The blue lights became a beacon that I followed. The ambulance was the object that now filled me with this sense of foreboding, engulfing me, restricting my breathing. They, the nurses tried for over an hour to resuscitate my mum, because she was only 64. I wondered how long they would keep on trying with Alan. I had not thought to car parking tickets and raced off with Cherrie to the Accident and Emergency entrance. We were let immediately through to be told they were waiting for a helicopter to take Alan to Kings College London. The result of the belt being placed around his neck had caused considerable brain injury and this is where he needed to be. I have experienced so many hospital corridors and so much bad news over the years, always delivered in a clinical fashion; after all it is fact-based, emotions are kept out so informed decisions can be made: 'Could I wait and they would get back to me?'

Cherrie and I did not cry, there were no tears now. It was as if we knew just six months before when we spoke to the police and shed all those tears. There was a sense of calm as we waited, holding hands, and just waiting. Then Nick arrived with Jonathon, I do not remember the sequence of events, the whole thing is a blur. Nick told me that, when he arrived, he just wanted to hold onto me and to Cherrie; and that is what he did as soon as he walked through the door, the four of us held on to each other. He had telephoned Patience as she had the children at home, and everyone was waiting for news. Staff raced through the doors to the room where Alan was while different nurses raced out and so the evening went on. Then someone came, I do not know who, to tell us Alan was on life support. There was considerable damage and a brain scan would need to be completed in the morning, they were waiting to transfer him to ICU and we would be moved to that waiting room. At this point two policeman asked to speak with us and offered to walk us round to ICU. They informed us that Alan was with his stepmother when he was dropped off at the station. Oh, my days! He must have been in for questioning and I was not contacted - the puzzle finally had the missing piece and the scene began to make sense. Then it occurred to me that we needed to contact people. Cherrie offered to make some calls and then mentioned we should probably try and find out where Alan's girlfriend lived. Facebook is amazing for this and in no time at all Alan's stepmother and girlfriend had joined us in the ICU waiting room. Emma was beautiful, dark long hair, pale skin, dark stunning eyes, and in floods of tears. Tomorrow she and Alan were moving in together. Tomorrow her life was supposed to start with this amazing man she had fallen in love with.

I turned to look at Cherrie, she had broken down and my heart shattered once again into a thousand pieces. Only nine months ago she and Alan had lost their dad suddenly, he was just 52 years old.

He was at the TT races when he collapsed. We received a phone call which left Nick and I taking out credit cards to pay for Alan and Cherrie to travel from Kent to the Isle of Man to see their Dad in hospital. It was a huge journey to take on so unexpectedly. Sadly, Keith died before they got there. At the time I said to Cherrie, there will be a reason for this, our Father skills us up through the tragedies we experience. Never would I have thought that nine months later she would be in the same situation, though this time with her brother. Now Cherrie was living the trauma all over again and I had no words for her, no hope to give her, only my love and at that very moment, even that felt insignificant. What right had I to call myself a mother when I could not keep my children safe from harm?

The two policeman that had walked us up to ICU offered us all tea, then chatted to Nick about possible foul play. Their words were wooden they meant little, we knew the circumstances that had led to this, the hole had been dug; we had been waiting for the final push. None of us could have foreseen that the impact would be so harsh, such a rip through the hearts of a family.

It's then that I drifted to every new scenario that I could fathom, all the variables, all the prompts, all the possible words; in none of them am I able to see people acting with a pure Christ like heart.

Jesus says do not go to the Judge, the law, the Pharisees. If you have a problem with family, you go to family. If you have a problem with a friend you go to that friend, you work it out, you act with Christ in your heart. We know Jesus Christ died for our sins, our Lord God sent Him because He knew how bad we were, how unable we are to change. It is human nature to interfere, and this is where we were, too many people had interfered and now Alan was on life support.

I walked over to the police officer to talk about Mara to ask if they had questioned Alan today; to tell them I had asked to be contacted - that three times I had asked the police to contact me, should they take Alan in for questioning. I know him well you see; I know how to reduce the anxiety of the unknown. Then another officer asked me if we could we talk:

Did I suspect foul play?

As we talked, I learnt that Alan had been dropped off by police that afternoon. He had been questioned, but there was no evidence for an arrest. In addition, enough pieces of the puzzle had been put together by the officers to rule out the alleged allegation. There was street cam evidence that provided proof of an alibi for the additional allegation of rape. Remember I said all the horrific words that sat with that. Alan was also supporting them with a case of fraud and was a key witness, so they had interviewed him for that while he was with them. He was in a good mood when they dropped him home. I visualised the scene, the amount of information Alan had taken in and knew this would have triggered his anxiety. The uncertainty alone would have left him reeling, the stimulus of bright lights and the transition from questioning to witness, all of this and more was sensory overload and would lead to an impulsive action.

Hours had passed, then we were finally allowed to go into ICU and see Alan. I raced down the corridor, I needed to set my eyes on him, touch him, let him know that I was there. Just as we do with babies who become restless in the crib, we place our hand, wide stretched across their small fragile bodies and gently 'shhh.' The contact is enough for the restless baby to know that they are safe. There was not one area of Alan that I could touch, tubes and machines surrounded him like a prison, a mechanical prison keeping him caged in. I longed to hold his hand, to be close enough to smell him, stroke his scruffy beard but all we could do was stand and look at him from the end of the bed.

'Okay' said Nick, 'we need to leave'. I have no knowledge of how long I had stood there, watching my son being breathed for. I turned to leave, right foot, left foot, think, think, think. Walk, walk, walk. Just do what comes next, open the door, walk through it, right foot then left, another door and another corridor - the cold 3am air.

What do you tell the children, the youngest two who idolise their brother, you give them hope because we still had hope? I prayed, I demanded and then laid awake and started to write THE WAVERN. I then planned ramps and wheelchairs, feeding tubes and respites. I was ready, and God was going to give me a miracle.

I need to check details at this point because as I have said they are all in the wrong order. It is as if the mind is unable to process such a traumatic event, and so places each moment in a jar inside your head, like the Numskulls from a 1970s comic. Then of course when you come to process them you see how jumbled up they all are, because the jar has been left, as painful things are best left alone, unseen, unsaid, locked away, and before we know it we are stuck!

We arrived back at the hospital early, not long after six, after no sleep. Belle was on her way and I remember being so keen to see Alan. The urgency was back, the same one you have on their first day at school when you cannot wait to pick them up. School might be out at 3pm but I would always be there at 2.30pm, excited to hear all the news, so pleased to see them, hug them, and breathe them in. When we arrived, we were asked to wait and see the consultant. Alan had been moved to a side room, he was no longer monitored by all the assessing machinery and finally I could stroke his face, straighten his bed, tuck his long hair behind his ears and tell him I love him so very much. Pass on messages from his siblings and chat about all the things we should have been chatting about but never did.

Then the consultant invited Nick and I into to discuss prognosis; he said words such as brain dead, tests, off switch, life support. I responded with donor card but that meant nothing as there needed to be an autopsy. 'What'? I protested, we knew what happened, he attempted suicide. But no, there were still unanswered questions about the day and so all we could donate was skin cells and other small soft tissues. This was the hardest part of all, after all we are told they are screaming out for donors, yet many are lost to protocols and autopsy. Why they could not do the tests while the person remained on life support is beyond me.

Nick and I went to find the Chaplin; right foot, left foot, walk, walk, walk. Do what comes next - open the door, let it swing, another corridor.

I did not invite the children, the younger two to see their brother. Their last memory of Alan was of him bouncing around at Christmas. I did not want them to see the life support system and a lifeless brother in the deepest sleep he had ever been in since birth, he never slept as a baby. Now here we are son, I patted his thigh, stroked his face, and kissed his forehead.

Oh Alan, Oh my boy, my dearest child. The Chaplin spoke a beautiful farewell, one of love and forgiveness, the droplets of holy water reminded me of the delight Alan found in puddles. Then the nurse unhooked wires and Alan slipped away with his own last breath, which was poignant as he took that breath, which told me had had heard us, he was there. He was surrounded by the closest of family and no more. We had only a couple of hours to sort things out and all I know is a piece of me died with him that day.

I know at this point God was holding me up with His righteous right hand, but I did not feel it, I did not believe it, I did not want to. After all, we all can have slippery fingers. God had dropped me, just as I had let go of Alan's hand, He no longer had hold of mine – or so I desperately wanted to believe.

We all went home, we cried and lit candles, we played with melted wax and sat for hours upon hours around the kitchen table and I carried on writing The Waven.

THE WAVERN

†
To the boy I look, to the boy I see,
I called to the boy, to come with me.
His hand pulled back, his eyes held fear,
the prickle of fright, bore a black tear.
Then the night scare, began to bleed,
oily scales, of hollow deceit.
For the witch, The Wavern, tied up in the air.
Her talons chorused, from her boned lair.
Whistling wind, spine chilled verse,
Japanese knotweed carried poisonous words.
Devouring soil, gaining pace,
the boy's porcelain hand, lathed his face.
The Wavern screeched her onset storm,
underlings grappling the grotesque form.
To the boy I looked, to the cavern I see,
as The Wavern snatched his hand from me.
†

My breath was lost held in fright,
a frozen haze in mid-flight.
There was no name, no soul to breathe,
no help no frame no capillary.
†

Lonesome now, the journey's named;
pursue the boy, The Wavern's game.
As knotweed crawls, violating the start.
Of the final beat, of a broken heart.
I entrench my foot, the labours choice,
no vocal cords, no words to voice.

Right then left, painful bones,
little steps the fodder moans.
The quest begins, the night scare broken,
as I pick my burden of isolation.
The Wavern cries, hold in the mist,
splintered glass seeps from the kiss.
She left on foliage, as she hurried past.
With the porcelain hand, firm in her grasp.
†
The skyline moves in blackened tar,
The Wavern's lizard tongue, holds no bar.
As she spouts her filth, to herd the beast,
that will haunt my breath, held in the heath.
The beast will follow and devour,
the feast of pain, I birthed each hour.
Lonesome now is what I see,
lonesome carries and walks with me,
grappling woods, living branches,
out to kill any breath with answers.
†
The Wavern screeches, flying past,
I look to the boy, beyond my grasp.
I called to the boy, I called to the air,
I called to isolation but silt lies there.
Congealed is the mud, that holds me fast,
no sense of time as moments pass.
Underlings scour from stolen nests,
built from memories taken from death,
meandering forms, dragging rumours.
The Wavern's torch of cancerous tumours.

†

Its then that the boy calls to me, a shattered voice in eternity
splintered, fractured, silenced, haunting.
Underlings running, The Wavern taunting.
the boy that she has, that' s not hers to hold.
There is no sleep, in this blanket of cold.
Lonesome still the Journey stretching,
echo' s run, memories etching.
In the mind sorting confusion
longing the nightmare, to be an illusion.
It was then the talons tackled me down,
into the amber, on the hot ground.
Through suffocating darkness, flailing arms splayed,
heavy and helpless I watch the boy fade.
From what I have known,
father God I wonder.
Obliteration approaching,
here comes the thunder.

†

Up from the amber, head up above the hell.
All-consuming night terror, all-consuming smells.
Burning pages of life as it passes.
Up rise the underlings the army advances.
Stench is the air from ammonia crawling;
sulphur rises as the smog continues sprawling.
The underlings crouch bent doubled back.
Calling out ' she' s coming' , The Wavern left her shack.
The Wavern' s left her shack!
The Wavern' s left her shack.
The boy is alone, I could get him back!

†

Blood begins to race, seeping from my skin,
the droplets form a coat, warming up my limbs.
I called to the boy, could feel him near,
lost in the sadness and fictional fear.
I called once again to ricocheted silence,
The Wavern exploiting emotional violence.
Evil and twisted she redefines a life,
thrilling in the turn, of her verbal knife.
Towering, the army chills me to the core.
Every bone in my body, holds a pain not felt before.
I look for an answer, that sees beyond tomorrow,
an underling strikes me, leaves a mark, a sign of sorrow.
†

I am empty, I am broken, a lifeless silhouette.
The boy is there before me, I have not used my chances yet.
I've not used my chances yet!
The night still carries moments,
I can rewind the regret.
I look to the path, I strain to hear a voice,
I strain to hear a breath, in this sunken pit of misery,
there is no time to rest.
I clamber and I crawl, as debris burns my skin,
melting and pungent, it fails to mirror the pain within.
Amidst the surrounding, there are shadows in the spaces,
tears distort my vision, what I see are simply faceless.
Hauntingly controlling, living hell holds so much ice.
Crushing my boneless body,
The Wavern has me in her vice.

Suffocating lungs filled with putrid air,
The Wavern holds my very being, I am trapped inside her lair.
Thunder rolls as waves of darkness strike me down.
Hell is looking hopeful as the air begins to drown.
Each gasp, each cough, each rasping cry, removing life from me.
I call to the lord to bargain my heart, yet even God can' t hear my plea.
†

For silence stifles every bone, each moment a brittle hour.
I long for the blackness to seal my eyes, I wait to be devoured.
Then nothing comes, there' s nothing left,
the mind and body feels possessed;
by bitter hatred, as she stands,
The Wavern swipes her underhand.
The underworld, the underlings,
The Wavern' s beast are carrying,
onward steps of colossal might,
the dark has no corners, to hide the fright.
The boy cannot run; there' s no way out,
from the mind that seethes.
Caught in judgments, dogma stories.
Drowning in The Waverns glory.
He lost his path, ran out of breath,
there is no clear vision within the mess.
The boy feels the weight of the aggressor,
then surrenders to the pressure.
†

I scream to the void that holds me fast,
I scream in silence the fear is vast.
As The Wavern thrashes, the world begins to break,
underlings scarper, from the immoral they escape.

I cry to the Lord, I cry to cross.
Sand is losing time the boy is all but lost.
I falter in my search, no meaning to my gaze.
The Wavern's deed is done; I have but one more day.
There will be no more nights, she has stolen all the dreams,
the days that were to follow have been slaughtered to the extreme.
The beast is now before me; time is running down clock,
motionless are the hands, as the body fills with shock.
I look to the boy his shadow I see.
The child and the man all but one to me.
I look to disbelief and disbelief looks back,
the beast has caused the panic and with the terror now attacked.
Rancid is the air, filled with putrefying sin.
The Wavern sent the beast,
to break the chain that held the kin.
The darkest days are merging,
rotting nights a time filled haze,
sleep eludes the broken,
the slouching beast brings slow decay.
†

Silence plays the drum, beats the blood flow in the ear.
Silenced is the heartbeat, weeping memories, ruptured tears.
I call to the night, I plead with any who will listen
the boy is there before me, mechanically imprisoned.
Hope has fused the moments, now the compounds breaking down.
The Wavern's vultures cackle out their stories,
their poison seeps beneath the ground.
Reaping what they sow, slander courses through the veins,
the Beasts ravenous mouth is open, the boy's life breath he waits to drain.

†
I call to the boy; he is so still, a blanket of black where nothing is real.
I look to the seconds, mapped by time, sleep erodes the tormented mind.
Along on trodden smog,
Underlings whispers carry hate.
The Wavern circles in the stillness,
a hollow bell rings out the fate.
The nightmare twists, taking turns towards the worse,
The Wavern wins the boy,
with a final demonic curse.
She has him in her cloak, a cage of feathered bones,
 the boy sits inside the darkness, far away from home.
†
It' s then that my Kin call to me, an army of hope in this misery;
it' s then that the few gather to clasp,
the pain and the love within their grasp.
For the beast has the boy, he is all but gone,
The Wavern delights in deaths dark song.
Dancing in her Kobi heels,
her blackened heart feasts on the Kin' s ordeal.
I cry with the Kin and they cry beside
the word of God and faulted goodbyes;
with sulphur thickening, the Beast does approach.
Speech is lost in the muted throat.
Spoken in the night, drifting on the breeze
God calls to the boy and he leaves with ease.
†
Anguish grips and sits with me;
anguish now a part of me.

Emotions run and rip the soul,
the spirit drowned, no longer whole.
Infinity stretches out the pain;
joy has gone from summer rain.
Thoughts that run at lightning speed,
the light is shining, and his soul is free.
The Wavern spouts high thrilling taunts
the prisoned boy a vision that haunts,
my eye, my gaze, the living hours.
The beast rampages and still devours.
Infected fury twists the depth,
The Wavern has not finished yet.
She stirs, she boils, the fetid lies,
feeding on the Vultures cries.
Breathing out, expelling dirt,
breathing in sweet bitter hurt.
†
Devastation rocks the ground,
no comprehension can be found,
to fathom out the players part,
to shatter still, the atom heart.
Devastation holds no bar,

its impact forages at the scar,
which the Beast made with it' s claw,
the mental state still so raw.
There is no calling, no name to mind,
to relieve the ache that' s left behind.
The missing piece,
the space between,

the gap,
the break,
the black ravine.
I walk the days, and along with me,
the shadows follow for company.
The Wavern here holds all the hands,
owns the deck of distorted plans.
Wailing in shrilling tones, pouring spite with her crones;
foulness hangs in dripping form,
from the squalor, the beast is reborn.
To hunt, to stalk, walk the earth
dispersing distaste, spreading un-worth.
There is no if,
no but,
its over,
the boy is gone,
he walks with Jehovah.
†

Here I am peering down,
the wearer of deaths murky crown,
twisting thorns, burrowing deep,
to deal with the pain that constantly creeps.

The sudden pang of perpetual emotion,
bereft the gap of maternal devotion.
I cried to the stars, for each word scribed,
I call to my God and he holds me fast.
Yet he can' t remove the momentous blast.
I gather the siblings to my breast,

we live in the moment, there is no rest.
Too many thoughts in darkened circles,
accept the pain will be eternal.
Accept the child, my God' s precious gift,
the love he had the days he lived.
Then grace the world with gratitude, let them in the magnitude
hear the words of simple adoration, expressive kindness in donations.
Read the countless effigies' , see the boy in all of these.
I look to the sea, its roar grips me,
crashing waves comfort grief.
I stand in the sand,
re-run time, hear the voice,
of the boy that was mine.
Watching moments, children laugh,
a mind fixated on this cinema.
I look to the court and there I stand,
the mother who let go of the hand.
I fall to the ground,
and then I fall again,
I pray to the lord,
for here comes the Requiem.

†

17
THE REQUIEM

There is a need to place the moment, perhaps in sensory form, of Alan's funeral. We had no idea how to approach this, how to finance this, how to deal with any of it. What parent does? There is no moment in parenthood that you think you will ever have to plan a funeral for your child. My heart goes out to all parents, worldwide who have lost a child at whatever age. The pain, feelings, questions, guilt, lack of control, loss of hope along with the complete desolation of the world you held so much faith in, all of it, everything implodes. Like a black hole pulling all you value in. There was an episode of Doctor Who that Alan and I really enjoyed called Satan's Pit. In that episode was a black hole, pulling in the stars and planets around it, the actual special effects were amazing for the time, yet the thought of something like that happening, really happening, formed ice around your beating heart. We were there, chilled at the task ahead. Then out of the blue the West Coast Bar in Margate for whom Alan did sound engineering decided to make contact; 'We would like to hold a tribute evening and raise money for the family, we had great respect for your son Alan'. I was astounded, it made no sense. The Red Lion were next: 'We have placed a collection jar out for Alan'; even blank envelopes with cash came in through the letterbox. We were still playing with candle wax most evenings, sitting together, drinking, talking, crying. "It must be a Tardis coffin." I announced, we can walk up from the Red Lion to the Methodist Church where Alan attended Sunday School. Steven the Minister told me that the church was closed for repairs but we could use the hall. This worked out well because Alan loved the hall. I used to be the weekend cleaner and we would all go to the hall on a Saturday afternoon.

Gertie would scoot around in the baby walker and Alan would take his remote-control car and create racetracks; later he would just play loud music and enjoy the space.

I remember little of the day, I held Rupert's hand for the best part of it, he was so close to Alan, our youngest, also autistic and struggling with the trauma of it all. He had become a non-speaking, non- eating boy, since the loss of Alan. We walked through town from Alan's local, an entourage of about 110 people, silently following a Tardis coffin up the high street, it was surreal. The coffin was adorned with lavender and hops and smelt incredible and as you walked past the coffin in the hall, tiny bits of hops would fly into the air and float gently to the floor, mixing in with the lavender smells. Alan was caried in by Ash, Little Pete, Nick and Jonathan, to the sound of Carry me, by the levellers. We sang at full tilt Shine Jesus Shine, as this was his favourite hymn. Then we played the Scarecrow at the end, by Coco and the Butterfields. I asked everyone who knew the song to salute Alan as we left the building – and they did us all proud. As the coffin went past, a 110 people stood up and saluted my scarecrow, my misunderstood boy, my Alan. As he left me for one last time, hops and lavender mingled in the air, a haze in the sunbeam and then no more.

I had not seen Alan much before he died, he always told me he was busy and I never believed him,

I put it down to the challenging relationship we had and it being the politest response to use. Then I learnt that he really had been busy, one lady told me how he had given up six weekends, to build her kitchen, because she had been let down. Another chap, told me an incredible story of his need to get sound equipment to London and how Alan stepped in at the last moment to drive him up there and then helped him out and drove everyone back... 'This is incredible' I told the chap; Alan never had a driving lesson and held no license! Another lady spoke about his commitment to her business and another about his ability to see such detail, before a project even started, so many people with so many stories. The outpouring of love and the amount of people Alan impacted on was on a whole other level. He had lived many lifetimes in his short amount of years.

2 Corinthians 4:17-18

For our present troubles are small and won't last very long. Yet they produce for us a glory that vastly outweighs them and will last forever! So we don't look at the troubles we can see now; rather,

we fix our gaze on things that cannot be seen. For the things we see now will soon be gone, but the things we cannot see will last forever.

18
EMMA

Emma was Alan's fiancé who came home with us from the hospital, sat with us round the kitchen table burning candles, playing with melted wax, drinking coffee with rum. Then a moment came when she needed to think about university, her house let had finished and she never did move in with Alan. Of course, I said 'Stay', 'Just for a term or two,' said Emma.

Emma, I am sure, went to finishing school. How else would she know that my cupboards had just enough ingredients to put a tea together should the prime minister ever decide to call? I was relieved to know this, after all it is good to be prepared. We chatted and giggled as we created all the possible scenarios that would bring the PM to my humble door. Farfetched were some, however Emma pointed out that most of my guests ended up staying here from farfetched real-life situations so I really should not rule anything out.

Conversation with Emma were often fanatical and fanciful, holding no bounds, creating inspirational ideas, and challenging the mind to all sorts of possibilities. A stunning dark-haired girl with beautiful pale complexion and curvy tall frame. Her intelligence was on par with Alan's and Rupert enjoyed chatting to Emma, discussing philosophy and other such conversations which always seem beyond my grasp. It did not take long to see why Alan loved Emma, on one occasion she came in from shopping and popped her tote bag on the table, dropping as she did so, tiny lilac lavender buds from the palm of her hand, the smell hit my nostrils and we both broke into tears. I was touched and lost; Alan had shared so many family traditions with Emma. I walked past her room one evening to hear the shipping forecast, something my mother had played for me to help me sleep as a child and I in turn had played for mine. I tapped on the door, 'Alan?' I asked and Emma looked up with tear stained eyes, smiled, and said 'Yes.' It was beautiful really, because having Emma here opened other stories and stories keep memories alive. They also allow you to see sides of people you did not know were there, how loving he was, the laughter they shared and the amazing projects he had planned. Yes, Alan would have made money, quite a lot of it.

If you gave a name to the first year of Emma's stay it would be called The Round Year, firstly because we ate and drank a lot. Cherrie, Emma, and I love food and all three of us stress eat. I baked cakes and they both cooked delicious meals. Secondly because we went around and around in circles with emotions, thoughts, feelings, and actions. Nothing worked, including the passing, and revisiting of the five stages of grief. The whole family was raw, and I am not ashamed of saying that I remember little; both of my youngest were out of school, both under CAMH's and both recently diagnosed Autistic.

In fact, this is important, I was working full time and Emma living at home with us was God's intervention. He knew I would need someone at home with the children, while I fought with the local authority to get them both into specialist provision. During this time Gertie-Grace received tutors as part of maintaining her education, she was extremely ill and diagnosed anorexic, not because of an unhealthy body image but due to extreme anxiety. One of the many quirks Gertie-Grace has is seeing detail and when faces are not symmetrical it absolutely causes her physical pain. There was once a news reader who had one eyebrow plucked slightly higher than another and when she came on to read the news, Gertie-Grace would leap up and exclaim.

'I can't look, turn it off please, quick!'

This particular week the tutor who was visiting had an unfortunate unsymmetrical face and wiry hair. A lovely lady I am sure, but these insignificant details were what stood out to Gertie-Grace and made looking at this lady extremely difficult. The other factor to fit in was the teacher's lack of understanding when tutoring a child who struggles with autism. This was commonplace in schools at this time and caused many parents with autistic children a lot of unnecessary heart ache, after all the right teacher can make all the difference. Unfortunately, this tutor read Gertie-Grace's anxiety as challenging behaviour and before twenty minutes had passed, Gertie-Grace was under the kitchen table and the tutor was raising her voice. Throughout tutor time Emma waited in the living room with the door open, on this occasion she walked into the kitchen looked at the lady who was insisting Gertie-Grace behaves herself and Emma announced; 'Gertie-Grace is right you are a very mean lady, I believe Jacqueline would like me to ask you to leave the property.'

The first year was disjointed for us all, the loss of Alan had not yet reached our radars and we all were continuously walking on splintered glass; still stepping over the rabbit hole - and then the first year passed.

Psalms 34:17-20 speaks about the good moral person who calls out for help; God will deliver them from their problems. I know without any wavering that our father wants only the best for us, and that he can heal our hurt, ease our hatred, turn our scars into a testimony. All we need to do is want it, to ask for it, to knock and open the door to the calling that is for everyone to hear. I feel that the journey through the thick darkness was needed. I remember hearing a post Easter sermon, about the two disciples who met Jesus on the road to Emmaus. What I had not heard before was the idea that maybe when we are in such a dark place, so deeply in pain, just as the disciples were as they failed to recognise Jesus. They still did not understand the magnitude of what was happening. Maybe, just maybe, this is our road to Emmaus, maybe that road, that place exists within us all.

Psalms 34:17-20

The Lord hears his people when they call to him for help. He rescues them from all their troubles.

The Lord is close to the brokenhearted;

he rescues those whose spirits are crushed.

The righteous person faces many troubles, but the Lord comes to the rescue each time.

For the Lord protects the bones of the righteous; not one of them is broken!

Let's get back to Emma... Emma has Italian blood and speaks with that passion, loves with that passion... Nick repeats the same conversation with Emma that he had with Sorello, and any Italian guest that comes in the house.

"What is it with all the pasta names, no matter what shape it is, it is the same filing and same pasta, cannelloni, its large meat filled with the same stuff used for lasagna, which is a large flat sheet that could be a tube layered with the same stuff that you make cannelloni with? What is with ravioli, its tiny pillows filled with the same stuff you make bolognaise with?" He would go on while Emma laughed and laughed and allowed Nick to finish his speech. She smiled her beautiful genuine smile that lights up her whole face and replied, "I know Nick, what can you do?"

It really was one of those moments where you must have been there. When Nick had this conversation with Sorello and Georgio, they became so passionate for their culture, it was beautiful to see. They defended their pasta and its many variations with a full-on debate and explanation; Nick hoped for so much more from Emma, and she bats it back with this curt cut short answer, I cried tears as I laughed, game set and match on the pasta conversation.

I remember the plans we had to decorate each room off the house, we spent a long while discussing it and never did anything about it. Then a time came when Emma desperately wanted the attic room and so swapped with Gertie-Grace. Gertie-Grace came downstairs to the room next to me and overnight Emma went from glamorous Italian student to DIY glam girl. I am not sure how she did it, she always, no matter what, looked beautiful. Emma's skin was flawless. I have only seen her eyes red and tired twice, once with an awful cold, which went through the family, and once in a hefty night out with Ash, this was after Alan.

Now here we were, negotiating five steps of bereavement touching up the rooms in the house, each day the sander could be heard and in beautiful queens English Emma would say, 'f**** this wooden floor, I did not think it would take this much work!' Her enunciation was perfect, which meant even cursing sounded good from Emma.

But she did it, turning the room from being just a bedroom, to a space that would look fab on the cover of Hello. Then Emma moved onto the sitting room, and that is how the year went, Emma finishing her Masters, and the house being spruced up. Emma fitted in well, we had bonded as family, maybe because 'great people are forged in battle,' this is not my quote but someone else's and I know - I got it from the Day of the Doctor, classic New Who. We all carried the same trauma, which provides common ground to build upon and we all loved Alan deeply.

1 Corinthians 1:10

"I appeal to you, dear brothers and sisters, by the authority of our Lord Jesus Christ, to live in harmony with each other. Let there be no divisions in the church. Rather, be of one mind, united in thought and purpose".

This verse explains why we were all able to settle down and live together while dealing with such trauma. We were cut from the same cloth, connected through Christ, and sharing this basis and my later experiences with Alpha ignited Emma's own faith and started her once again on her journey back to God. But before that journey, rather suddenly in the middle of the second year, Emma took to job hunting at the coffee house. The painting ceased and we watched with as much curiosity as the cats who live with us, her comings, and goings. This was a brand-new move, the first of many new moves which would wake us all up. It was time for us all to climb out of the dark and deal with the hurt. Emma had not gone anywhere, none of us had gone anywhere for over sixteen months. We loved Emma and wanted the best for her, we figured it must be a man, after all they have a way of turning up eventually.

Of course, by week three of Emma's job hunting, I had to ask what the pull was in the coffee house, after all It cannot be all good coffee and Wi-Fi.

'Well,' said Emma, 'there is this chap, with a sort of Viking Nordic look about him,' and there it was, the confirmation that there was a way out of the dark.

Ombre had a way with the ladies, charming them with his gentle smile and boyish charm. It was evident that the coffee house did as well as it did because Ombre's way of asking if 'they wanted extra cream with that?' melted their hearts or caused their uteruses to skip a beat. I could not see it, my eldest daughter could not see it, and I am sure there were some who were immune to it, but not our Emma! We all felt that this would be the rebound guy, the expendable one. You know it must happen to enable emotions to be worked through, but no love is lost and it is a relief when the relationship breaks up. Sadly, Emma invested a lot of her time and effort in Ombre. It appeared he was 'the one.' People questioned me and my feelings over this, after all she had been engaged to my son. I had no worries, I loved Emma and wanted her to know that and to know she can love just as deeply as she had loved my Alan. However, I was struggling because as much as I wanted Emma to move forward, Ombre was not the chap I saw her moving on with.

"You are batting too low Emma." we told her,
"Ombre is definitely batting too high." We finished with.

But still the feelings grew. I decided I needed to remind myself we cannot help who we fall in love with and of course God knows the plans He has for us. This was Emma's journey and not mine, holding onto that we went along with it and committed. This Commitment saw Ombre moving in as he had been made homeless by his landlord, all to do with no water and other needed amenities. Following the Lord's word, his will is not easy, it means we are challenged to put away our differences and even our belief system, and this meant I needed to hold back on any comments made by Ombre. Nick however, stated he was not a Christian and could say what he pleased. Which bought about another thought; there are good people out there who are not Christians, and bad people who are Christians. Using the term Christian does not make you a follower of Christ, it is your actions, which will speak the loudest. Nick still had to be nice because he been raised with good morals; you must put away your differences. It is what good people do - it helps the world go around when we do not bring in our personal opinions.

Ombre enjoyed gaming, so we did not see him much and started to see more of Emma. On one occasion Ombre was left to sort his own meal, and all he cooked was three steaks. I laughed and laughed as I revisited Gavin and Stacey and found myself repeating the story of Three steaks Pam... I suggest if you do not know it, to look it up.

On another occasion, Emma was cooking a meal for herself and Ombre. The lamb chops were under the grill and Emma was a little cross with Ombre, but we did not know why. Just as she pulled the grill pan out, Pond, our spaniel, appeared from out of nowhere and grabbed one of the lamb chops. 'I am so sorry,' I said through shock and laughter, 'It's okay' said Emma 'to be honest, Ombre only deserves one chop anyway.' Had I managed to grab the chop from Pond's mouth, she would have put it back under the grill and served it to him; he really had stepped over her line! We were never sure what had happened, and no sooner had the line been stepped over than there were candlelit meals, Channel perfume and whispered sweet nothings. The line was back in place and Ombre remained a part of the home.

Then it was time for our Gertie-Grace to have her first three-day trip away to Disney land Paris; she was so excited. Cherrie was taking her with her BFF and they both were so excited to take Gertie-Grace on her first girl's road trip. We always took great delight in each other's achievements and this girlie road trip had been planned in detail to allow for each autistic anxious second that Gertie-Grace might experience. Of course, the return of my girls after their three-day trip, would usually have had me at the door waiting excitedly for the news, the pics and vids. Instead, as I prepared for their arrival there was a sudden wail of emotion and Emma was standing at my bedroom door in floods of tears.

"Ombre says we are finished, I cannot believe it, I thought we were doing fine".

We sat on my bed and I asked where Ombre had gone, after all I did not want him in my home, not now he had upset my Emma. The tears continued, the hurt was not really Ombre related; yes, it hurt to be dumped, it hurts more when you do not get to be the one who does the dumping. None of these were the issue. What had happened was Emma was experiencing another loss and so because she had yet to deal with the loss of Alan, her default response to hurt was to relive the grief she felt when Alan died. The tears had become a flood gate and then the key turned in the front door.

I raced into the hallway to see Gertie-Grace and Cherrie in the doorway;

There was no welcome, instead a quick gesture as I encouraged both the girls into my bedroom as Gertie-Grace heaved in her trolley case...

"Ombre has just dumped Emma". Both my girls came to offer comfort and get all the details.

It broke my heart to be the one once again wiping away tears, to see anyone you love so to upset awakens a passion deep inside to protect. Once Emma had gone upstairs to wipe her face, I sat waiting to see if Ombre was going to come back. I was so surprised that he did, bold as brass as if he had done nothing wrong. I asked him why he was here? He looked all innocent and said 'I am going to bed.' 'What! You break Emma's heart and think it is okay to remain in my home? Uh no, it is not okay, you need to give me your key and leave.'

'But I have nowhere to go!'

'Well, you cannot stay here, my concern is my daughter and you have chosen to remove yourself from that equation, you need to leave.' I am pleased to say he did leave, and I snapped the chain onto its hook as the door shut behind him. Behind me my daughters clapped and for a moment I felt as if I had become a character from a scene in a Jane Eyre novel.

It was after this that Emma took to decorating our tiny living room. It was never something I had asked her to do but it had been something we discussed. I had the paint and Emma had the skills and so for five days we had no access to the living room. I felt a pang of loss as the week took shape and Emma's focus so fixed.

"She's leaving". I told Nick.

"You don't know that." Nick said to me.

But I did, I felt it in my heart, I felt the lump in my throat form a bitter round ball of salty tears. It was to be the end of an era. This moment of time, where we cried so much and together, walked a journey of brokenness until our wings healed and the Lord allowed us all again to fly.

Do you feel the Lord's love?
Journal here!

19
EMMA'S STORY (TOLD BY EMMA)

On my first night at the house, Cherie brought me back from a local bar where I had been marinating myself in whisky. I stayed in Rupert's room, cried into a cat, and slept. To invite someone, you have just met to live with you is a difficult thing during the best of times. To do that when you and your own family are experiencing the most excruciating and bottomless grief imaginable is another thing entirely, but that is precisely what this family did. We agreed that I would stay for "a bit". A bit turned into "the year" while I finished my studies. The year turned into "two and a half to three years, give-or-take a few good months". I was immersed in a supportive environment, full of people willing to share themselves, their traditions, and their home, and all the ordinary things were special. Coming downstairs and being offered coffee, being introduced to recipes and comfort foods, watching favourite films, decorating and singing 4 Non-Blondes songs at gloriously antisocial volumes. I think it would take me a whole book to come close to describing the time I spent at the house. There were tears, and deep existential misery, but at the same time there was so much laughter. It was often hilariously, side-splittingly funny. I laughed so much I left with toned abdominal muscles and eye-wrinkles. These people have some comic timing and abstract humour that would make many working comedians take notes. They have this buoyant spirit and down-to- earth nature, and they are tremendously creative and original in addition to being huge-hearted, patient, generous, and warm. Know that they all dress phenomenally well, and they are hilarious.

The house itself is a perfect match for its family. I do not think God had to think too hard to bring them to the right location. It's typically Georgian, in a small crescent of old townhouses, overlooking a picturesque library just above the centre of town. It is a pocket of old-fashioned charm in a sea of modern buildings. The house is tall and slender occupying the corner of the crescent, and a large wooden staircase stretches from the living room in the basement all the way up to two bright loft rooms three floors above. The ceilings are high, and the walls are crammed with original artwork books. A row of thick wool military jackets hung along one wall, and a row of ballroom dancing dresses hung along another. I had a great front-facing room downstairs with a view of the library out of an east-facing window, but when Gertie-Grace wanted to swap, I very happily relocated to the front loft room. I asked Jacqueline if I could paint it, and she not only said yes, but didn't even raise an eyebrow when I came back to the house with six tins of various shades, sandpaper, filler, brushes and rollers, and proceeded to give every square inch of the room at least three coats for the right "airy" effect.

On the first floor there is a long hallway with a door at each end leading to either the garden or the street. Some genuinely smart person thought (rightly) that it would be an idea to put a small loo in this hallway, a little square-ish room with enough space for a lavatory, a radiator, and a sink. Some other smarter and more creative person thought (rightly) that it was about the right size and shape to be painted like the TARDIS from the iconic sci-fi series Doctor Who. The old wooden door and frame went a deep rich blue, the sign on the front had been put on, and the windows painted in. The inside had the appropriate number of round things on the walls. I don't know if you know this, but it is actually impossible to come home and not laugh at that fact that you're peeing in a Tardis, no matter what kind of evening you might have had.

On certain days of the week, things were different. On Sundays

Jacqueline would fill the house with the smell of fabulous home-cooked roast, cinnamon rock cakes, or bread and butter pudding.

Saturday evenings were for Fish and Chips and watching Doctor Who. This combination is about as comforting as it gets. If you cuddle a cat while eating Fish and Chips and Watching Doctor Who, you are experiencing the maximum level of comfort that physical reality can provide. As a person who had always distracted myself from my thoughts, I had not really had much practice at making time every week to do comforting, feel-good things like watching charming TV with great people and cosy food. It was new to me. I now know that food, family, and film, is a winning self-care formula that should be applied often. I learned that it's important to enjoy simple pleasures in life, and that you must make time to practice them. I still do this, and I advise Fish and Chips and Doctor Who as a recipe for happiness.

Jacqueline is an amazing person. She is a huge-hearted force of good, and she stands up to unfairness, wickedness, and stupidity wherever she sees them. She understands without judgement, and when she gives a person advice, she sees them as a unique individual, and considers their feelings, and values. Jacqueline is vibrant, creative, loving, honest, fair, and funny. She also knows what she is talking about. She prayed with me, and we stood in the front bedroom in the house, and asked God into my life. She showed me how to speak with God, and how to go about finding the peace I had been looking in the wrong places for. She gave me the best dating advice I have ever received, a chocolate cake recipe to bring out when I need to impress someone, two saris, and an endless amount of patience. She also cheerfully took me food shopping, on a Sunday morning, while I was more hungover than I had ever been in my life. It was a hangover of colossal proportions, and every photon of light was sharp. The tweeting of birds sounded like industrial machinery. The sound of my own breathing was like nails on a blackboard. I leaned out of the stationary car and wished for death. Jacqueline didn't judge. The shopping arrangement had been decided some time before the wine consumption, and we were going to get the job done. In one hour, Jacqueline had planned a week's meals, found all of the ingredients, selected the best vegetables, remembered all of the things she had been asked for over the previous week, met Sam and helped her with her own shopping, packed in order of coldness and checked out, all while dragging my (largely useless) self, up and down the aisles dispensing kind words. I am still in awe.

Rupert very quickly became one of my favourite people. He has one of those brilliant brains that instinctively understands complex mathematical principles and feats of engineering. It's possible to watch him thinking about something, and actually see the parts slide into position in his head. He'll then be struck with surprise that whatever thing he was thinking about is actually not so complicated after all 'Oh!". Then on to the next thing. As acquiring new information comes relatively easily to Rupert, he has amassed encyclopaedic knowledge on all the proper subjects, i.e. he knows all the fascinating little details about the things that interest him. What interests him? Interesting things of course. Supercars, prehistoric life, animals that will kill you, and sci-fi, are among the most genuinely fascinating attention-grabbing things in existence, and listening to someone explain precisely how the breaks work on the latest Bugatti is one hundred times more entertaining than whatever it is that you were doing. Many successful Youtubers know this and have developed careers accordingly. Rupert also understands humour on another level. He has this look, and it's absolutely fantastic.

Gertie-Grace was the usual recipient of the look, but anyone who deserved it would receive. If you said something truly and exceptionally dense, you would get the look. This look was not merely disdain, no. Too obvious. The look was something like disbelief that you just said something so unutterably moronic, followed by pure amazement that a person's brain might entertain such a laughable thought, and finally joyous mirth that the person in question not only thought something so profoundly thick, but then said it out loud. Then that sharp mind would slap back with a retort, like a champion tennis player serving a devastatingly fast ball with terrifying aim. Amazingly, Rupert did this all with a playful easy charm, it wasn't serious or hurtful, it was sport, and watching it was the best spectator action I've seen in a long time.

For a few reasons- all of them bad- I was sharing my loft room with a chap. I would describe him as a four-letter man, and all offensive four-letter words apply. This man once fell down the topflight of stairs in the house at around midnight while carrying a litre and a half of Canadian maple syrup.

He was paying no real attention to where he was going, fell, dropped the syrup, smacked into a wall, and damn near knocked himself out. By the time anyone was able to work out what all the noise was, precisely all of the sticky pungent liquid was dripping its way down and around the colossal staircase that connected all four floors of the house. Jacqueline and Nick demonstrated the patience of God that day. The syrup had reached the kitchen on the bottom floor in approximately seven seconds.

It was on every bannister, it was on the cats, it was dripping down the wall. It was running in shiny dark rivulets down every handrail and on to people emerging below, the smell was delicious. The mess was everywhere. The loud clattering thump shook the whole house. Jacqueline reacted first to make sure that no one was hurt. Nick emerged sleepily followed by other semi-snoozing family members. Instead of the volcano-like reaction I had in mind, Nick blinked a few times- "maple syrup, needs warm water", before heading downwards to pitch in to the extraordinarily generous collective cleaning effort. I aspire to that level of calm.

Gertie-Grace is an excellent creature. She called me Kevin for at least the first year I lived in the house, and I felt it on an essential level. I became Kevin. I embodied Kevin. Gertie-Grace is the little sister I never had, and I do have a younger sister. When the maple-syrup man left the house, we stood in the hall as he carted off the last of his material possessions. I knew that if I said anything, whatever came out would be offensive, so I kept my mouth shut. Jacqueline waved, and, being the amazing person she is, wished him "God bless". Gertie-Grace stood in the doorway and finished "and good riddance". I love her. She can spot someone talking absolute rubbish at 100 yards, and she is supremely wise. On a less-wise occasion, we decided to make brownies and found a recipe on the internet. Me, being overly ambitious while totally lacking baking skills, looked for "best ever gourmet five star brownie recipe" instead of "easy dependable idiot-proof brownie recipe", and the two of us made a trip to Waitrose for premium Belgian cooking chocolate. The flavour was similar to dirt, and they had a definite soil-like texture. The mixture looked like compost before they went into the oven, and they smelled bitter and acrid from the start. We wondered if that is what all brownies smell like and assumed that during the cooking process the heat would miraculously transform the brown goo into delicious dessert. Obviously, that did not happen. Both of us tried to eat them, but they were indescribably revolting. I had fun with Gertie-Grace no matter what we were doing, and I have honestly never laughed so hard.

There was a tiny table and chair set on the roof terrace balcony, and I sat there and watched a taxi pull up to the house with Johnathan sitting in the front seat. Odd. He got out of the car, went round to a back door, and proceeded to pull a huge antique filing cabinet out from where it was wedged into the vehicle. The cab driver looked deeply confused, gratefully accepted payment, and sped off. Apparently, he had seen it in a local antiques market, and thought it would make an excellent storage unit for his room on the top floor. It was a characteristic design, and look, it is such good quality, they don't make them like this now. To give him credit, it is a cool piece. The corners are rounded, it has a pale blue-grey enamel finish, and it is almost as tall as I am. I say "is" because it's so heavy, and the trip from the pavement up the steps to the house and then up three more flights of stairs was such a feat of physical exertion that I don't want to imagine it making the trip back down. He'd seen it a day or two before, and thought he'd better snap it up before someone else did, so he bought it and worried about getting it home later. I do not know how he managed to get a cab driver to take it. That is a level of persuasion I have never been able to achieve.

Johnathan had this cat called Potter. He was a compact muscular creature with wild fur and glowing yellow eyes. He resembled a wolverine in character and appearance, and he was a furious fighter.

Potter came back to the house to eat and sleep, and he would hiss and claw at anyone who was not Jonothan. He liked junk food, and would steal slices of pizza, after Jonothan taught him as a kitten to hunt pieces of steak off his fork. Everybody else had to stroke him wearing oven gloves, but Jonothan could coo his name and make a soft clucking noise, and Potter would climb up his clothes and sit on his shoulder purring.

Johnathan also had a girlfriend (now wife) Turophile, and the two of them were basically a package.

They have been best friends since school, they have too many in-jokes to count, and they have this effortless, comfy, trusting ease with each other that comes from having grown up and evolved

together. She also let me draw on her face with makeup and didn't mind that it took me two hours.

In an unlikely-yet-possible collapse of civilisation type scenario, I would choose to be in Cherie's bunker. She is an excellent judge of character, she suffers no fools, she is fiercely loyal to those she loves, she's thoughtful and sweet, and she will cut you if you cross her. Cherie is a born survivor, capable, resourceful, and powerful. If she has your back, you are an incredibly lucky person indeed. She is carefully selective, and she has great taste in all things. Clothes, décor, food, people, places, it honestly does not matter what it is, she can identify the gems among all the rubbish. Whatever Cherie is doing right now, she's doing it to a high-standard, and with an original and sophisticated perspective. She is adaptable and can turn her hand to anything and succeed. When I think of Cherie, I remember her fixing her classic mini, in a great outfit, with a toolkit and a Haynes manual. She's down-to-earth and charming, and she creates memories with, and brings joy to the people around her. Her siblings adore her for so many reasons, and I would definitely and whole-heartedly support Cherie for president.

It was a gorgeously warm weekend in early summer, and everyone had been spring cleaning for a while already. A large aluminium garden shed had been selected, and this construction was generously sized and very reasonably priced. A location in the garden had been chosen, and Johnathan and Nick had spent the best part of a morning flattening and preparing a square patch for it to sit on. A few giant cardboard boxes had arrived, and the website boasted that assembly was easy and uncomplicated. Suspicion crept in when Nick opened the leaflet of instructions and found that it was 80% pictures, and that the drawn images that were supposed to resemble parts of the shed had been sketched by someone who had definitely never seen the thing in real life. There were a few lines of text to describe how the thing should go together, but they were in German. We flipped to the back of the manual to see if there were any more instructions that were not in German. There were. In Korean. At this point, everyone should have given up and returned the thing, but we thought the shed itself might be alright. There were a lot of pieces, all numbered, and the manual did show which numbers comprised each section of the shed. Nick is a mechanically minded individual, used to fixing pretty much anything, but after two full days it became obvious that it wasn't going to go together. There were no holes where there were supposed to be holes. The parts that formed the shape of the roof were much too long. There were holes where there should not have been holes. The manual said that we needed to assemble each section of the shed separately, and then simply bolt each bit together, but the corrugated window-less base looked like a soviet-era water storage tank, while the top looked like an aluminium tepee. The only person who could have fixed the situation was Jacqueline, who rang a man from the company and explained to him in no uncertain terms that if he did not take the shed back, there would be a divorce and/or a murder. Fortunately, it fit back in the boxes pretty well, and after some cursing and some hideous shrieks of metal-on-metal, the monstrosity was gone.

Nick is excellent at fixing things. He is a person who makes the world better task at a time, and his children are especially lucky beneficiaries. He also possesses zen-master levels of calm and quiet unless something really deserves otherwise. During the time I was there, Nick discovered a real talent for custom-creating theatrical outfits inspired by Edwardian and Victorian aesthetics and incorporating modern punk design elements. Steampunk clothing can look jaw-dropping but to achieve a unique look, it is necessary to do the sewing yourself. That is exactly what he did. Nick sat in the kitchen hand stitching gold trim to jackets and altering hats and creating fascinating decorations with watch parts. His stitches were tiny and evenly spaced. He used threads that were pretty much invisible, and he was selective about what would go well together. The effect was fantastic. After mastering fabrics and fashion, Nick turned his attention to interior design. We had given the living room a couple of coats of paint, and I had done some filling and floor painting. In doing so I had piled all the furniture in the centre of the room and moved the pile to whichever half was dry. Jacqueline had set us the task of having the place finished by December 1st so she could decorate for Christmas. On the Morning of December 1st there was still a huge pile, a stack of pictures to go on the wall, furniture, and accessories still in boxes. Nick rounded up the occupants of the house and gave us tasks with military levels of planning and organisation. The aim: to transform the living room from a paint-splattered storage room for a mountain of stuff, to a cosy and chic lounge with interesting and glamorous accessories, before Jacqueline came home from work. We would be bringing back the 90's TV trend of one-day interior makeovers, but this one actually had to look good. Masking tape came off, curtains were studded with those horrible plastic curly things and attached to curtain poles, pictures went up, books were stuffed on shelves. Nick vacuumed frantically as the clock counted down to five o'clock. Herringbone throws were draped over sofas, new cushions were plumped and arranged, lamps were found for mood-lighting, rugs were unrolled, and everybody listened for the dogs to sound the alarm. Rupert and Gertie-Grace took care of some final-second finishing touches and Nick brewed coffee with minutes to spare, and made it look like we had had the whole thing under control all this time.

A good chunk of time after first moving in, I loaded a small mountain of my personal belongings into a rammed car and departed. There were many long hugs and kind words. I was hugely sad to be leaving, but enormously and entirely grateful to everyone for accepting me, being so kind to me, supporting me, advising, consoling, comforting, laughing with, and sharing with me. Moving out felt like leaving home for the first time, or like birth all over again. I arrived a mess of a person, and I left with a support system, a fledgling relationship with God (still fledgling but working on it), amazing memories, belief in myself, healing, and a fledgling sense of inner peace (wobbly, but present). I had the experience of living in a loving family, and feeling like there was someone to turn to when everything was going wrong, someone who would celebrate with me when something was going right, and someone who'd laugh and assist without judgement when I'd done something exceedingly stupid. Living in the house absolutely gave me an idea of what great relationships and a great family dynamic look like, and what divine love and acceptance looks like. I gained so much love in my life, and I am in no doubt that God put me there.

Emma's story completely blew me away when I read it and it bought to mind the intensity of the time we shared and the trust we had as a family; tucked away in the skinny house. I was reminded by a dear friend of Ruth's commitment to her mother in law and I feel this reflected Emma's journey, taking her steps of healing alongside my own.

Ruth 1:16

"But Ruth replied, "Don't ask me to leave you and turn back. Wherever you go, I will go; wherever you live, I will live. Your people will be my people, and your God will be my God."

20
JULES

Jules is laughter on a sunset evening, carried across on the wind, she rides the honesty train and holds on fast despite jolting from those who are determined to shake her belief. I want to say she is accidently ours, but I know God has a plan and incredibly Jules is a part of that plan from the moment the seed was planted. I love her, I literally cannot do anything for her. Her independence is the force that gets her up each morning and motivates the deep clean of her home, which is as pristine now as it was when she first moved in. Jules can nurture and mother, she can be the sister needed in the tearful moment and the boulder required when we look for strength. Jules is a phoenix that can uplift all those who stand nearby, yet if you look deep enough you can see the sadness behind the eyes and cry a lake together, just because. I had known Jules for maybe a year, she is a professional hairdresser. We decided we would go to the closest salon to our home, which is literally eighteen houses away. Cherrie would have her hair done and we, as in Gertie and I would chat to Jules, Nicole with the immaculate Bob and little Nicole, who always did Gerties hair. It always turned out to be an end of week therapy session, I loved that about the salon, the comfortable conversation that developed after becoming accepted regular customers.

I am unsure at which point one becomes a regular customer. Is it after regular visits of four or more, or after four visits are you still just acquaintances? Whatever the amount of time needed we had surpassed them all and friendships had formed. Then one sunny afternoon immaculate Bob Nicole announced she was pregnant, later that afternoon I overheard Jules tell Cherrie that her mother was ill with a rare type of cancer and how she felt so helpless, with no understanding of how to respond and what to do next, on top of everything else, Jules continued, I am pregnant. My heart reached out there and then. I am a fixer, there is this ridiculous piece of me that pushes my feet into action, before any thought of how to help, has entered my head. It often makes a fool of me and I am often left apologizing. But on some days I am left thanked, with a grateful heart of gratitude and the fixer in me can relax.

Our visits remained regular and the splashes of colour in our hair continued to change with each visit. Jules has the same skill with colour as Van Gogh does with oils. Colours are expertly painted onto strands, by the end of the three-hour visit you leave looking completely vibrant, awake and modern with incredible hair. Each time we visited the hair salon it was obvious with Jules ever changing bump that the pregnancy was fast taking shape it seemed to be the elephant in the room, Jules was in complete denial that this small mound in front of her was going to actually be a baby. A human being that needed feeding, Bathing, nurturing, and cuddling...then repeat.

Cherrie, who was similar in age would ask, have you looked at prams yet? Clothes, cot, packed a bag? To all these Jules would say, no. her no was clear and blunt, it said discussion over, not that there was ever a discussion. Instead we chatted about trips to London, her Mums treatment, and the new development of a changing relationship between mother daughter. We also endlessly chatted about her brother's antics and her little sister Jenni. Jules carried a weight of pain for Jenni, she had no answers and was unable between work and pregnancy and mum to be the sister she wanted to be. Instead Jules became the mother figure and with that started the 'Battles of Wills', every injustice held by a teenager along with the right to do as I want, was fired at Jules, we watched her grip the hand rail of the honesty train and spin at a 100 miles an hour. I can honestly say at this point, so close to baby being born, Jules was a phoenix about to burn.

The first we know of the birth of Jules daughter was on face book, a small perfect baby with hair, ginger hair, much like her fathers' beard. The fact that Jules might have a ginger haired baby had not occurred to her, Jules believed her baby might hopefully be bald and the acceptance of a 'ginger' baby, could be processed gradually as the roots grew through. No chance, there she lay in the arms of her father a beautiful daughter with stunning red hair.

Jules is the only mother I have met who went back to work within an incredible short amount of time, it made sense, she was always at the hospital and Baby was either travelling with mum and Nanna or staying with Nanna while Jules worked. It was a beautiful thing to listen to; the play dates Baby had with Nan. The ability to bring distraction, love and emotional healing to a very poorly lady – such a beautiful clever little baby. Jenni also supported the childcare team and it appeared to me that God had managed something rather amazing; a connection between generations that on any other foundation, within this family, would not have happened.

On one of our visits, Jules whispered in Cherrie's ear, then Cherrie whispered to Gertie and finally I got the message when I got home. Jules felt paranoid that the manager was going to make the decision to sell the shop. After all she also had a daughter and running a shop with overheads that cripple into the childcare budget, was making the decision rather easy. The news was not a problem, the problem was, what should Jules do? My response was selfish.

"Work from home". I did not consider the words...can you, would you, may I suggest. Nope, just fact and fear about who would do my hair, who could I trust to place pinks and blues and cool tones onto my roots and turn my brassy blonde into a work of art? The answer was nobody, there really is not an expert to outshine the skills of Jules. Sadly, moving takes money and time, time is precious and Jules mum was deteriorating health wise and despite earnest prayer, needed a stem cell transplant.

It is hard to watch suffering, to see illness and disability take its toil on people we love, on anyone. It is not Gods plan to inflict pain on us, what he will do is take our suffering and equip us to cope, to find something beautiful. Jules had a relationship with her mum she may never have had experienced and her mum, for a few seasons had a relationship with her granddaughter, and she adored Baby.

The week that led up to Jules mothers passing was heartbreaking, Cherrie and Gertie and I cried most days, we knew the depth of pain about to come and we knew we could do nothing to prevent our dearest friend from hurting. Then later that month, weeks after the funeral we heard a joyful Baby ask to go and visit Nan in her garden. The simple faith of a loved child, no doubt in her mind that Nan is in heaven, watching in her garden. How we all need to take note from that simple faith. Jesus said the kingdom of heaven belongs to the meek, not the weak, but the meek, the kind, the gentle, and the peaceful. I believe also the faithful, the trusting and of course the believing.

Time passed; Baby was talking. I am unsure what age she was although she could easily be an early talker. I would not be surprised, as Baby reflects Jules, this child has been here before, her wisdom and responses are spectacular, her imagination far out does any Disney movie. Her role play and ability to mimic scenes from her favorite films are totally precious to watch. There was a moment one year when Baby thoroughly enjoyed home alone. I opened a video in What's app and there was this mass of mess in Jules hallway – it was as if she had been burgled, objects from the dining room and kitchen were piled high and Baby was climbing over the bannisters and stretching her small frame over the piles of objects to negotiate herself to the other end of the hallway, then in an accurate American accent she said;

"Merry Christmas you filthy animal!" I laughed tears, I truly watched that video over and over.

It was not till Jules bravely undertook the Tree of life tattoo on her back, (because her mother whole heartedly believed in its culture and heritage), that I realized how much faith Jules mother had; the tree is seen as a symbol through many cultures and religions and holds different meanings but it seems as if there is a common theme; A Connection to Everything, It symbolizes togetherness and serves as a reminder that you are never alone or isolated, but rather that you are connected to the world. Through Jesus Christ we are also connected to the world. I understand that the tree of life represents rebirth and through Jesus we are born again and promised eternal life. For me I have also felt a great sense of peace with trees and my own mother taught me to go up to a tree and place my hand upon the rough trunk, pause and breathe and feel the great sense of peace as I stood connected to the universe.

One afternoon my phone vibrated and our little What's app group notified me of a message and there were the words from Jules that were to form a forever connection:

"I am officially an orphan." I read the words several times over and I cried. I could feel her grief and the loss of identity.

I responded how you would expect me to respond,

"Then we officially adopt you". And there it was, a simple moment, which for one week only I ran with. I wanted a party, a welcoming, a certificate, a speech, I wanted to throw so much love to Jules and her daughter. I was voted down, Cherrie and Gertie rightly said that I would scare her away. So, we never spoke of it afterwards, the party became metaphorical. Instead there is an acceptance that we are family by choice and that takes a lot of work and recognition.

Most recently Jules had a mental health crisis and acted completely out of character, she somehow ended up agreeing to have a kitten. Oh the journey and the stories have only just begun; this little black Cat was named by Baby who is now in school. Baby decided quite rightly that he should be called Prince George and with Covid rules as they are, it was Jules who stood on the vets top step and was asked loudly have you come to collect Prince George? From there it has been helter-skelter, the idea of a cat is vastly different from owning a cat, cats are selfish creatures who need to own the human and not the other way round. Prince George is no exception and went immediately to work on the man of the house and Baby, he wore them both down quickly and won his place on their laps, their beds and of course their hearts. Jules was going to take longer to win over, so Prince George decided it would be in his best interest to mark his territory in the house, so Jules knows he has made his claim and he loves her;

"Mucking cat has peed everywhere!" are the words on our chat but with a F instead of a M. "Why has he ruined my life, as well as my furniture?" the sentence continues.

"Oh dear", we would emphasize.

But for all the heart ache and lack of experience, you know it was the right thing to do when Jules lost him and painfully took her beautiful home apart to find him. He had gone, or so it seemed. Then five hours later he appeared from the inside of a chest of drawers and the relief from Jules was that of a person who somewhat likes Prince George.

Jules is adopted into our family;

we love each other because of who we are and no more. There is no expectation, no rules, just simply being together, we share the highest of moments and the most awful lows, we climb into the hole to empathize with each other and occasionally we all jump on the honesty train and scream as we grab the rail and hang on to our beliefs.

When I think my journey with Jule's I am reminded of how often this beautiful woman will try. Everything is done with perfection to an end goal and she will not give up, not until she knows there is nothing left.

James says it well in 1:2-3; he speaks about counting the joy, seeing each challenge we have as Joy, which it is when we know it is for the Lord. This joy and gratitude for our life experiences produces determination and commitment in our faith journey and I feel that this approach of 'steadfastness', works the same way when applied to relationships.

James 1 2-3

"Count it all joy, my brothers, when you meet trails of various kinds, for you know the testing of your faith produces steadfastness."

21
THE GOODNESS

Psalm 31:19–20

How great is the goodness

you have stored up for those who fear you.

You lavish it on those who come to you for protection, blessing them before the watching world.

You hide them in the shelter of your presence, safe from those who conspire against them.

You shelter them in your presence, far from accusing tongues.

The purpose of this chapter is to reflect the goodness of God, the healing of God, the grace and mercy He gives freely, which has allowed me to climb out and recover from the dark depths of the rabbit hole.

Within two weeks after The Wavern, I had initiated a complaint with the police; after all, I had mentioned three times in a recorded telephone call that I needed to be contacted should they ask Alan to come in for questioning. The complaint entailed long drawn out forms and a timeline for which I had no measure. I stated that there was no transition between the two successive interviews, one referring to the historic abuse and all the horrific words that sit with that and the other as a key witness to a huge fraud case. I knew that the environment of the interview room would have created further trauma and there would have been no adaptions to language used, bright lights, no explanation to body language of officers who did the questioning. I knew also there was no autism training to understand the body language of the interviewee, no understanding to mental health and I imagined no mental health assessment.

I waited weeks for a response from the police, Alan's funeral was the 15th April 2015, we were still waiting for a coroner's hearing on the first anniversary. I believe it was June when I was visited by a female officer who had been assigned the complaint. I was unsure what to say, I felt overwhelmed, none of us had processed the loss. I was still looking at my phone in the hope that Alan would text me, still turning the corner and catching my breath as a lanky young man with Alan's gait would wander past; I was still doing 'what comes next'. The only purpose of the initial visit from the police officer was for the flood gates to open.

The clock on the wall showed that three hours had passed, the kitchen table was strewn with tissues and empty teacups, it had been more like therapy. The officer hugged me, said how sorry she was and that she would come back with her findings.

Meanwhile, I had been retriggered, I was a complete mess and did not know how to start to fix this. It goes without saying that my GP had already sent my children to CAMH's (Child, Adolescent, Mental Health) for me though there was basic counselling and huge waiting lists for anything else. "Why have you not gone back church?" my father questioned. Now this could be God my father asking; but in fact, it was my Dad. We had a challenging relationship; he had listened to Gossip and not to me and the odds were stacked against us having any kind of relationship. Clearly God had a different plan and here we were, my

Dad, reeling after a particularly unkind fall out with Mara, which gave us the opportunity to move forward.

> Genesis 19:17
>
> "As soon as they had brought them out, one of them said, "Flee for your lives! Don't look back, and don't stop anywhere in the plain! Flee to the mountains or you will be swept away!"

This verse mentions escaping to the mountains, although I know this verse refers more to Lot and his wife, it speaks about God's compassion when destroying Sodom. Yet it is significant as we hardly deserve this compassion if we continuously look back to what was then. My Dad and I were here right now, and I needed someone, for I had been disowned by so many. It was as if past events were played out and designed by me, my only part was to be the mother. I had not instigated anything, yet still I appeared to be the accused and a sentence had been cast, while I was not even aware there was a case against me.

> Luke 9:62
>
> "But Jesus told him, "Anyone who puts a hand to the plow and then looks back is not fit for the Kingdom of God.""

This sits well with me, I can see the visual; for if the ploughman looks back while making the troughs in the soil, the lines will not be straight. The ploughman has to keep looking forward, to keep the furrows straight. If you are going to follow God you need to keep your eyes fixed on the future and the prize at the end, the Kingdom of Heaven. A

Christian cannot yearn for what once was, pleading that everything was better back then. We cannot hold onto our friend's behaviour from yesterday, even when yesterday happens to be fifteen years ago. We need to forgive as we have been forgiven and move forward in Christ alone.

I listened to my father, and in fact to the wise words of the bible, I needed to move forward only. There was no point being so cross in the Lord. I was angry and bitter, we had lost my grandmother and then mother, in the space of nine months. We then lost my mother-in-law, then Keith and nine months after losing Keith, we lost Alan. I was angry. I did not understand and the only way I was going to understand was to have a conversation with God in His house.

There began my search for a church that would meet my changing faith. My Mother, God bless her, had an incredible faith and over the years of our time together I had been taken to many different types of churches. After Alan, I would drive around the towns after work, numb with hurt, a desolate grief and a need to connect, to feel something.

One evening I found myself outside St. Augustine's, I had been confirmed here when I was ten years old. My mind replayed memories; morning lessons in the monastery opposite, with Father Patrick. I remembered the difficulty I had in 'signing the cross' and being told a visual cue to help me; spectacles, testicles, wallet and watch.' If I had been able to put my slowness of learning down to being autistic, maybe it would have helped, I am unsure. The fact was, I found it hard to retain and the visual clue given was one I took literally. Which meant I spent most of my confirmation lessons wondering why I needed to point to testicles when I did not have any, and when was I going to get a watch!

I associated bible stories with a feeling of love and warmth and I honestly found a sense of peace and a uplifted spirit after we had said prayers. Of course, these memories were from childhood and I imagine somewhat distorted, or maybe as a child the love was more sincere? I do not know, but on lighting a candle as I walked into the church, I quietly took a seat and wondered at the coloured glass drifting its rainbow onto pews and clothing. I listened to the service and took communion. As I came to bench, along with the act of bending my knees to kneel, I felt a pull, a call from God. After the service I went to ask the Father who took the service, if I could take confession, to my surprise he did not have time and asked for a brief introduction from me, prior to booking some time. I was overwhelmed with uncertainty and fear, it was not supposed to go like this, I needed embracing. Instead, I was told off, how dare I take communion before confession, especially as I had not been to church for so long. My feet carried me out quickly, right, left, right, left, right, left. As my final step hit the pavement I breathed, and the tears rolled down my face; with my back against the cobblestone wall, I felt completely hopeless. I wanted to shout.

"Where are you God? you have taken my Alan and now You leave me grieving, cold, numb and alone."

I am unsure what time I went home, I fell into bed, stayed awake all night and went to work in the morning.

Another week, another church, no welcome, no eye contact, just me feeling awkward as I realised, I had sat in someone else's seat. I went home unfulfilled, unloved, alone, and still searching.

One late summer morning the police officer came back, her news was unforgiving, as I was told that there was no evidence that the interview process could have triggered any trauma to Alan; I was not happy, this was not what I had expected, I should have been called, my phone message should have been acted upon. I cried as I listened, silent tears from my eyes, dripping into my teacup as I held it up to hide my face. Then unexpectedly she informed me that she had watched the interview; and mid-way through Alan was telling the officers that this was ridiculous, that his mother would have something to say about this, she was a fighter, she never let anything go until there was an outcome that fitted her expectation. His mother was a storm to be reckoned with.

I listened to this, so thankful to hear my son's words, albeit second hand. Our relationship had been rocky from the onset, fueled by trauma and the naivety of first-time parent. By having Emma at home with us, I had seen firsthand the family traditions he had shared with her, reinforcing that he loved these and remembered these moments that stuck in my heart. Now here I was, held down by strong grief, being told that my son knew I was a fighter.

1 John 3:14

"If we love our brothers and sisters who are believers, it proves that we have passed from death to life. But a person who has no love is still dead."

We are being told in this verse to love, not just to love but to truly love, which Christians know as Agape, which is a selfless, self-sacrificing love for other people. It's a love we are driven to act upon and I knew I could not let this go.

Then it happened, another 'God incidence'. An open door from the lord.

One of the young people I worked with through my self-employment needed an appropriate adult, due to being questioned at the police station. I prayed so hard that this would go well, that this young man would be safe and okay. That I would have the right words to use and the strength to do what was right. Unbeknown to me, this was all God, He had given me what I needed to make a fight for change.

This young man was terrified; he had stood in front of an overpowering reception desk, which was raised and appeared to be there to intimidate. The officer quickly read his rights and at the end asked if he understood.

"Yes", the young man responded. I looked at my charge and asked the question differently. "Do you know what the officer has just said to you?"

"No" he replied.

There was the first piece of my argument for change.

From the desk we were led to a bright white room, the fan was on and it echoed with an annoying vibration that your mind would fixate on. My second piece of the argument that the environment is not right for those with trauma and or who have mental health issues.

The walls of this room were covered in a pegboard type material, bright white with tatty scruff marks. The chairs were cold hard plastics and the officers spoke into a recording machine to say who they were and the number of arrests or prosecutions they have made.

The officers asked questions in quick procession, no time to process each question the officer asked. I would interrupt by holding up my hand, in a stop sign, breathe and ask the question a different way. Still the officers appeared to intimidate, bringing fear over compassion to the whole interview process. My third piece of evidence for the long battle ahead.

From there we were taken to a room to wait, so we waited. The room was cold, the desk had messages scratched in it, that were not positive for a vulnerable person to read. The lawyer who had arrived had no understanding of autism and basically told me that he should plead guilty immediately. My argument was that this young person had no idea what they had been accused of because they had no script of understanding for the situation, they were in.

My fourth reason to follow further my complaint and fight for change.

After my time supporting this young man, I telephoned the officer who was helping me with the original complaint; we spoke about my recent experience and finally I had enough evidence to make a complaint; Alan was right, when I find my voice, I keep on at it, until I get the outcome that is right for those with out a voice.

The cry of a wounded animal reached my ears, it was one of desperation and it had escaped my own lips.

'My Alan, my boy, I miss you so much.'

My time now was not mine, it belonged to work, it belonged to the complaint to family but not to me. I was not letting go, the rung of the ladder began with local officers meeting me and listening to the evidence I presented. Soon enough I was met by Captains and delegates who would support the need for change. Still, we had not had the coroner's hearing, and whilst I also chased this, in hindsight this was all part of God's plan.

First though I needed to find a church, a place to feel embraced, I had lost sight of me, I was partaking in half a bottle of wine most nights, often without a meal. The loss of Alan was still not on my radar. My youngest two children were not in school, and if life was going to find a normal or improve on the old, it needed a miracle.

It was Christmas 2015; well, the end of November and everything was a 'first', the first Easter without Alan, the first celebrated birthdays without Alan. Alans birthday arrived and we sent of a flourish of balloons with messages attached, up they floated, taking our prayers and messages to heaven, to Alan. The whole year was all around the 'first' and now Christmas was fastly approaching and I was an emotional mental wreck! My dad had told me to try the Salvation Army. He had been thinking of his mum; a wonderful, small, dark haired lady named Happy. Happy had been a Salvationist and Dad told me to go to a service, after all I had tried everything else. So, I went, with two reluctant children in tow. I decided to hide in the stalls, upstairs, firstly because people with autism prefer to be out of the way from the masses and secondly, I felt awkward and was ready to be rejected again. Instead, the lieutenant who ran the church, found us. He came up and warmly shook my hand. He could have said, 'we do not use the upstairs,' but instead he chatted and told us all about the carol service the following week. I really love carols, it is the first sign that Christmas celebrations are on the way, then of course it is followed by the Christingle; the children creating their orange into peace and light.

The service I now sat in was a challenge as I had not thought about the brass band, and as they hit the first few notes, the sound bellowed up through the opening circle and we were baptized by notes of fire! It was beautiful, I tingled, I felt warm for the first time in ages, I felt God embrace the whole of me. The children felt overwhelmed and needed to leave. I continued to go to the Salvation Army and in the New Year people were invited to attend the Alpha course, this is when I felt the goodness of God.

Psalm 107:13-14

"Lord, help!" they cried in their trouble, and he saved them from their distress. He led them from the darkness and deepest gloom; he snapped their chains.

(During Alpha) My testimony

A nightmare for all of us generally is a place we desperately need to wake up from. When in deep sleep we will struggle as we wake to discern what was real and what remains a definite part of our dark mental state that needs to be locked away out of sight. My nightmares had become my living days, my waking moments were shaped around all my darkest truths. The challenge I had, was to find light in my days, because there was not even a faint beam bouncing as if it reflected off a silver teaspoon. My nights were drifting moments of no sleep, where my thoughts weaved a tangled web of disparaging affirmations, which were added to the burden of baggage that was my day. I carried these around like books stacked in a leather book strap, I willingly looked at these twisted affirmations and built them into the profile I had become. Pre-grief I was someone else, now I was a shadow of my former self. Literally a shadow, grey in face, waxy skin with limp lifeless hair. Conversations were stilted and often confrontational to match the affirmations I wove at night.

I lived, I took part in school runs and I battled, I fought tirelessly with the police to change the rules, to look at protocol for those with poor mental health. I wrote to leaders and to the local authority; these letters were either based upon getting my children into specialist provision or continuing the battle for change. Between all of this was the mundane list that can be a saving grace for some; cook dinner, do the washing, walk the dogs, pay the bills, fight the battles, and stay sane. Come on, do not lose the plot the now!

I was however losing the plot, I felt as if I was in the early stages of dementia. This was new and it was scary. How was I to address this nightmare? I was unsure if my dreams were reality or my reality my dreams; nothing made sense. I did not make sense, I needed help and with that knowledge I rang my GP. This sounds simple but just as it is today, so it was a few years ago. A telephone call for health care takes time, takes you through various recorded messages and directions and takes you through a process that often leaves with the phone call being disconnected. The actual appointment to see my GP took a while, as I battled through being tenth in the call queue and hanging up and trying again on another day.

When I eventually saw my GP, I was attending week four of Alpha; How can I have faith? This was when Jesus really rocked the ground I was walking on. Alpha that week was all about prayer, why should we pray? What should we pray? Is there a right or wrong way to pray? Of course, the answer is to just have a conversation, and if you are not the talking type, then use the words from the Lords Prayer, which is of course how Jesus instructs us to pray. Well, those who know me, know I can chat. I am no expert and my words and my conversation threads are often continually muddled. But talk I can do, and by the end of the session I was in tears and praying my heart out.

'Take my life Lord, it's all Yours, here I am Lord, use me for Your work'. Heal me Lord, remove this pain from me and let me bloom only for

You. Amen

I cried after that, I sat with Josie as she prayed. I knew then that God was calling me to join the church, be a Salvationist, wear the uniform and of course the hat! I knew that all efforts from me to be a Christian before now, were fake, I was the Sunday Christian, I knew God, and I had tried, but not hard enough. Jesus knows my heart and I know that if I am authentic, my heart needs to do a lot better. I bowed my head and promised God that I was going to be dedicated, committed, and put Jesus at the center of it all.

It was after this revelation that I experienced five days of shift; the first was in me, I physically felt it. I had shifted, like the earths' plates, there had been movement in me, a transformation. No big bells or full song musical, I knew I was different. I knew I would never be alone again, that I walked with Jesus and I needed to trust in Him. I certainly was not finding it easy, the week before my decision I supped on an evening glass of wine, now I had moved to herbal teas. Somehow though, I really wanted this change, I felt a drive in me to be a better version of myself every day.

The second day of shift (between battling schools and educational reviews) was a telephone call confirming the date for Alan's coroner's hearing. This was the start to later change; the hearing of course unwrapped a lot of hurt, re-triggering trauma. It turns out grief and bereavement look more like an infinity loop, rather than a process of boxes and feelings you work through till you are done. I am still to this day being caught out, catching my breath as a new wave of hurt, unfelt before, travels through my senses and threatens to pull me back in.

The coroner's hearing included the questioning of the officer who had listened to my recorded telephone call, requesting three times that I be contacted to support Alan, should he be asked to accompany any officer to the station. When asked why he had not contacted me; he replied simply that he did not feel it was necessary. The hearing was an afternoon event and God's answered prayer. The ruling from this hearing was that Kent Police needed to train front line officers in understanding how to recognise Autism in those undiagnosed and how to respond and alter language used in questioning, when interviewing anyone with poor mental health. This result caused a ripple effect through Kent Police and I was invited with other parents to Maidstone Police Head Quarters to discuss which content is best and what type of training should be offered. We all felt that face to face training works well when speaking about Autism, and that whilst front line workers needed to be prioritised, there was a need for blanket awareness across the force.

The third shift was totally unexpected, another loss for my youngest son who was attending a Special Educational Needs school, which happened to be where I also worked. We had an appointment for his review, and as far as we were all concerned, all was well. Sadly, no sooner had we sat down to the review than we were informed that they were no longer going to support his place. My heart broke into a thousand pieces, Rupert had just lost his brother and now after finally finding a school where he felt safe and had built one clear trusting relationship, he was going to be moved. I could not breathe, my heart was having palpitations and my skin had gone cold, I needed to leave, I needed to collect my son, and walk out of the building. My husband followed me. and I telephoned KCC, in fact I telephoned many people. Rupert deserved an apology and I handed in my notice. Our two- parent income reduced to one overnight and I believed that God had deserted me, because I was full of sin. I had a list of wrong choices attached to me like your skirt when it fails to fall into place after you have been to the loo!

The fourth shift came that week at Alpha, as I poured out my heart to the group. The good and the bad, a definite feel that God was in control of life as I clearly was not. Our lieutenant asked if we were interested in signing up for 'Soldiership' classes and this was the focus I needed, in fact it really was the one thing I could be certain of in a world with so much uncertainty, Jesus needed to be at the center of it all.

Being out of work allowed me to reevaluate what it was I needed. I needed, I explained to Nick, not to work for a month or two. We could afford for me to take six weeks off. I need time to reflect, re- think and rejuvenate. I could help the church sort out the literal quarter ton of recycling, spend time supporting food bank and working out next steps, this was to be the fifth shift.

I was at peace, for the first time in a long time, spending time in God's House was healing, spending time with God's words was rewarding, refreshing, revitalising and all the other 're's'. The six-week break from work was now six months. Nick had decided that my God clearly must have plan and as one of the three atheists in the family, he wisely let that plan play out. So, I continued to be out of work and Rupert continued to be out of school.

I misjudged how powerful you are...I think we all do...you transform lives, including mine.

I was extremely humbled, to be back again stepping out in faith, trusting the Lord with all of it. This was gift given to me, to see that through being so busy at Church, I had stopped interfering in all things school. I stopped an awful lot of things. Instead, I prayed a lot and others prayed for me. It was then Rupert was offered a school place and

I had secured some self-employed work, this work would secure our finances, albeit tight, for another year. Through this time, I ached to be back in church, I felt such a pull to be involved in full ministry. My work finished and I began again to support the church and this time I was offered employment. Praise the Lord, for I knew this discipline would see the best of me and my walk with the Lord.

Then it happened, what everyone warned me about. I saw Alan, I saw Alan in the gait of the young man walking past on the opposite side of the pavement. My heart wrenched as I saw Alan in the long scarecrow hair of the chap who bought in a clothing donation. There he was, unexpectedly on television, in magazines, in the conversations I had with the children. It was like a montage of Alan, a live feed before my eyes, spilling out all that he was to me and to the universe. My hand at these moments would cover my mouth as my face crumpled and the flood gates opened. The tears fell, but this was different, the pain had gone. Seeing Alan everywhere was almost as if God was reaching out to tell me he is okay, he is safe and where he needs to be. If I put it down to mere coincidence instead of a God incidence, then it was reassuring, I see him because I remember him, I hurt because I loved so much.

Jerimiah 17:14 is a powerful verse, it tells us clearly that when we commit to the lord and we promise his will, will be done, not our will. Then we receive what we read in the Word. We will be saved, for we praise his name, we will be healed because everything can be achieved when we trust in God.

Jesus tells us that he will heal us, he will restore us.

Jerimiah 17:14

Heal me, Lord, and I will be healed; save me and I will be saved, for you are the one I praise.

And the people all tried to touch Him, because the power was coming from Him and healing them all. 'Because I will restore you to health and heal your wounds, declares the Lord.'

Then just as my faith had taken this leap and just as I may have drifted with life's distractions, God sent My American Brother, his story is told after Curly's.

Psalm 31:19–20

How great is the goodness You have stored up for those who fear you. You lavish it on those who come to you for protection,

Blessing them before the watching world.

You hide them in the shelter of your presence, Safe from those who conspire against them.

You shelter them in your presence, Far from accusing tongues.

Reflet on the good...
Journal here!

22
CURLY

Curly caught my heart the moment I worked with him; he was a part of the shift in the previous chapter, where I was offered self-employed work, in my role as Children's Champion when I was unemployed. A young man of sixteen with poor organisational skills, social anxieties, continuous misunderstandings of expectations who struggled to manage life. He 'loosely' borrowed money and of course loosely being the term that describes the lack of knowledge from the lender and the lack of the funds being returned. Curly struggled with all the autistic traits. Despite this, a consultant in his wisdom withdrew that diagnosis of him. I remember the image that went into my head as I processed this news. It felt as if the government announced a new policy that will reduce NHS waiting times by a national half; this will be achieved by removing your diagnoses and pretending you do not exist!

I mean how can you remove a diagnosis that is clearly there and how can one elderly consultant do this without a team of people and another assessment? Enough of that! Once I get on a topic that I am passionate about, you soon will find that the horse I climb is indeed exceedingly high.

Autism is difficult to diagnosis because you must have always had those traits. Many of the traits can come into play through Adverse Childhood experiences (ACE's) and Post Traumatic Stress also has similar symptoms in some areas. In Curly's case he was a Looked After Child who had experienced probably 6 plus ACE's. However, when looking through his information it was clear he had struggled from early infancy and yes, he was still autistic.

I thoroughly enjoyed meeting Curly, who mostly sported the 'J-GOOB' look, probably because he had 'Just Got Out of Bed,' but it suited him well. He always listened and he always nodded in all the right places - when he was listening. His understanding on how he needed to respond in social situations was spot on, for most daily events. Sadly, he listened but did not hear, he nodded but did not understand. The moment I left, he forgot the one task that he had been set and went on his merry way. We would meet up each week and each week I would find that the despite unpicking events and scripting strategies, he was at this point not going to develop. I wondered if perhaps he had reached his limit of growth and understanding, that he would remain this cute fourteen year old, taking risks and managing to underplay every serious event in his life, simply because he had a head of curls, the sweetest smile and the ability to charm the people he met.

On one visit, I discovered that Curly had had a party in his flat, (which he had just about managed to keep a hold of). The neighbours had complained and I went around to check on Curly and to do some damage control with the landlord. As I walked in, I could see immediately on the cream smooth walls, that something had dripped from ceiling to floor. I walked and turned slowly round the center of the room, yes, whatever it was had dripped down all four walls. I stepped over takeout boxes, cider bottles and various Gin bottles to reach for a cloth. I wiped a spot of whatever it was, it would not disappear. I walked to Curly's room and he was out for the count, I prodded his bare foot that hung out of the quilt, with my booted foot, nothing. I prayed he was not dead. I poked him and called him, still nothing and so I placed my phone next to his mouth and thank goodness the phone screen reacted to his breath and hazed over, I breathed a sigh of relief and started to tidy. Two hours later as I finished removing alcohol from the flat to the boot of my car, Curly had woken up and was standing in a towel looking at the tidy flat and then looked at me.

I waited for the Sorry. There was always a sorry and the flash of his smile and then the story. How he did not know the people who came in and partied. How he had said a friend could drop his coat off and said friend came with said others who gate crashed in and had a party. In between his story I asked had he even thought about asking them to leave. Curley replied that he had tried, but by that point the neighbours had complained and he felt ill. I explained ill is usually from bugs and virus's, what he felt was the effects of alcohol and it was commonly known as drunk. Any time after the drinking has stopped it is known as a hangover. Curley was no first timer to the impact of alcohol and my response to it, I enjoyed teaching the lesson and ensuring I spoke loud enough that it hurt.

'Thank you for clearing up', he said and reached out his arms and I leant in for a hug, I could not stay cross for long. Why would I? It is not like I was never young and never made foolish choices, in fact age is irrelevant, I still sometimes make the wrong choice.

The soft spot I have for these struggling young men, is because of my own struggles with Alan. I completely understand why they respond the way they do for the reasons they do and of course when you serve those in need, God gives you the ability to love them unconditionally. I loved Curly, he had my heart; after all we had shared so many conversations and I had been there for most of the recent 'solution focused' meetings. These were with his social worker to rectify the complicated situations he found himself in. However, being solution focused was insignificant to the love life of Curly. He caught many a girl's heart with his charm. I have lost count of the broken hearts that closed his front door in the six months he had his flat. But all good things come to an end and Curly's inability to pay his bills meant it was time to leave. Social Services informed the fostering agency they would not help this young man and so of course he ended up at ours, just for a week or two, until a place of support could be found.

When Curly arrived he was dating Sharon, a lovely girl whom we only met briefly and who was only going to be a 'brief encounter' in Curly's life, as she was heading off to join the Royal Navy. Curly needed love and long distance was never going to work, but at this time he was determined to make it work. From the children's point of view, particularly Gertie-Grace, Sharon was a good name for an assistant. This is a quote from Rowan Atkinson's sketch as a vicar and just as Eliza had become a quoted line before, so now would Sharon, a good name for an assistant. Curly would walk into the room and either Gertie-Grace or Jonathon would ask.

'Where's Sharon?' then follow with 'that's a good name for an assistant that is.' Curly would smile and I would laugh, as it is all in the delivery. Gertie-Grace is a delight to watch, continuously making us laugh. Curly appeared to attract minor scale incidents and on one occasion he wandered down looking completely lost and announced he would struggle to stay in if he is unable to play his PS2.

I enquired why he was suddenly unable to play games and he informed me in a matter-of-fact way, that he had been cleaning and the TV had fallen and smashed. The crack in the screen was deep enough to know there was no chance the broken tv could be rectified, fortunately we had an old tv in our room and donated that to the Curly good will fund.

I had initially wanted Curly to stay until his funding ended; however, it was a challenge to secure the funding and I was unable to commit to long term support on rent alone. So, with a heavy heart Curly moved on to supported living. In that time Sharon and he broke up and then the girl of his dreams arrived, with love in her heart to give and a place to stay out of area. This was the push Curly needed. When we spoke last, he was feeling settled, with a sense of authority in his voice he spoke about the plans he had for himself and his partner and the baby they were expecting. I think about him often, living the day to day and pray that he has what he needs now to feel happy and at home.

> 1 Peter 5:10
>
> "In his kindness God called you to share in his eternal glory by means of Christ Jesus. So, after you have suffered a little while, he will restore, support, and strengthen you, and he will place you on a firm foundation."

This verse is from one of Peters letters, and it is reassuring as he is telling us that yes we will suffer in this life, but for those of us that believe in Jesus Christ and have faith, they will be restored, renewed. Being a Christian is not a freedom pass to an easier life, and for those Christian who are persecuted, it can often mean death. Through Jesus and the cross we have the promise that through eternal salvation suffering will end.

How does God guide you?
Journal here!

†

23
MY AMERICAN BROTHER

The first time I met My American Brother was when he stood up in church and gave a short testimony and ended it with; 'If you wanna listen guys, this brother could do with a brother to talk to'.

My American Brother was from Chicago, I know there is more detail than that, however I struggle to retain all the details so am unable to tell you the exact location he lived in before he came across to England. I can tell you that he spoke in a soft Chicago accent, which was smooth to the ears, plus My American Brother delivered his thoughts with care so always spoke slowly. In short, My American Brother has a voice for audio books, lovely to listen to while being soporific enough to allow you to drift off to sleep. It was after My American Brother told his testimony that I introduced myself, saying;

'Don't just ask for brothers, you have sisters to'.

We chatted and My American Brother told me that his mother was English and had lived in Maidstone before moving out to the States to marry his father. My American Brother had arrived here in England nine months earlier but was now going to settle in the South East as he enjoyed the community of our Corps.

My American Brother lived in a beautiful old building that had been a Special Needs school for many years. This building faced the glorious seafront of Broadstairs and across the road is an expanse of green stretching out as if carpet cloaking the sea. Beyond the green and railings, there was the sea with its tones of blue to green, some days swirling its anger and crashing onto the shoreline, a stunning view whatever the weather. In contrast on a hot still day the sea was a quiet as a mill pond, gently rocking the boats as if soothing their occupants of to sleep. You would think it would be hard to leave, wouldn't you? Unfortunately, no, nothing is as it seems and this was no different. Yes, it was all beautiful, but the managers of the building were shocking, My American Brother was left with no heating and no proper cooking facilities. It was the lack of heating that was of the most concern. It was January and no matter the location, cold is cold. Then despite alarms, youths managed to get in to his flat on more than one occasion; living the dream My American Brother was not. What made this more of a Challenge was My American Brother's poor health. I will not complicate the story with all the details, but, in a manner more associated with a hospital bed, My American Brother would connect himself up and manage his own transfusion every week. He would also need to use a gadget like a nebuliser. My American Brother would sit breathing in this life changing mixture, when he paused to look up or to talk to someone white smoke would leave his mouth and he reminded me of the caterpillar in Alice in Wonderland, wise and all knowing.

At this stage in this story our spare room was occupied by Curly and I was unsure how long his stay would be. All I could do was pass on an electric blanket and with the rest of the Church Family, pray. Prayer is a wonderful if not sometimes a questionable practice, only because when we place our hands together in prayer and come to our Lord with our requests, we really do feel that what we are asking for is the right thing. We think hard about our need, yet some of our prayers go unanswered and we wonder why; or they are answered and but it makes no sense in the situation. This of course is down to our Father providing for need and not for want. He sees our long-term needs? while we see the now.

He ensures that from the unpredictably of life that He can give us something new. Our Father's agenda is never to cause pain, He knows how that feels, He gave His Son, and He heard Him pray:

> Matthew 26:39
>
> "He went on a little farther and bowed with his face to the ground, praying, "My Father! If it is possible, let this cup of suffering be taken away from me. Yet I want your will to be done, not mine."

Our Father does not make the bad things happen; what He can do though, if you ask and trust Him, is give you beauty from ashes.

As a church we were all praying and almost as quickly as the prayers left our lips Curly moved on and My American Brother moved in. No sooner had My American Brother moved in, than the building he had lived in was broken into again and a fire started. My American Brother lost the possessions he left behind to collect later, but as he said, 'I am safe.'

Again, I remind you; all in God's timing.

I am truly blessed to have Nick as he had not met My American Brother and had not really heard me discuss him that much at home either, as he had been working in Scotland. Nick is a laid-back Yorkshire man, which is why we complement each other well, Nick has always said that the reason My American Brother was allowed into our home was because My American Brother like me, was a Soldier in the Salvation Army. This Nick believed was bigger than a DBS check, as he had seen the discipline needed to be a Soldier and felt that this was a good measure of the man he had gone to pick up.

He was not wrong, My American Brother was a gentleman, extremely grateful and quirky enough in character to fit rather well into the family, though it was not an immediate fit for the children. It is always difficult when you have a guest in your home but add the social challenges that autism creates, it then makes it so much harder to adapt to new people, to know how to respond and of course the change of routine again.

When I look back, I see that not only did God bring people to our door who really needed time to heal or a space to develop and grow, He always sent people with the right balance of character. There was rarely awkwardness, though of course I acknowledge Ivy outstayed her welcome and it was difficult - which only reinforces the age-old quote: 'You can't choose your family.'

My American Brother and I quickly became friends and spent an awful lot of time discussing how to improve the services we offered at the Salvation Army. My American Brother, like me, volunteered a lot of his time. When he arrived at our home, he was quite unwell and not able to walk much more than twenty-five feet. I am pleased to say that after six months this distance and My American Brother's health had improved greatly.

If I were to describe much of My American Brother stay with one word it would be quietness.

Jonathon would share YouTube videos with him, while My American Brother would educate us with his favourite cartons and pieces of music. My American Brother's mother was English, so Gertie- Grace took on the task of breaking his accent and started teaching My American Brother English pronunciation. This was funny as whenever Gertie-Grace was about, My American Brother would ask for tea, working hard to speak the word clearly and ending the word quickly.

The American drool does seem to stretch the word out, elongating it somehow. I am no linguistic, but My American Brother learning to speak with an English accent always delighted us all.

Another simple pleasure in having My American Brother live with us is his love of good food. My American Brother enjoyed food and like me had a sweet tooth. Within the first two months of My American Brother's stay he mentioned how much weight he had lost since living here in England and that he needed to put it back on for his clothes to fit! Not the usual approach to weight loss and it really made me laugh, 'No, no, no you buy smaller clothes!' I exclaimed through my giggles. Despite the weight loss I am pleased to say My American Brother always was thankful for my baking sessions. These usually happened when I was stressed and always ended up with enough to share. The house would be full of warm air and the smell of spices travelling up the stairwell to My American Brother's room. Yet he always came downstairs, unassuming and ask, 'Have you been baking, is there oatcake?'

'There is, I would say and My American Brother's face would break into a smile. I called this smile the oatcake smile and imagine it to be the same as the smile on a small boy's face who is offered the beaters to lick once the batter is made. It is a pleasure to bake for someone who is so appreciative.

My American Brother has a strong faith; he is the example that you need to keep trusting. The hurt this wonderful man has experienced is a mountain high, no difference from the hurt that many people feel. It was this hurt and some early teen experiences that shaped his faith and eventually drove him to England - well he flew, but you get the picture. No matter how forgiving we are we do not forget, but our memories take us by surprise at times and the trauma is experienced again.

One morning when I went downstairs to start the morning routine, My American Brother was up and he was having one of those low days, reliving the trauma. Most of us function better in a relationship. We are better people when we are accountable to the person we love. We might make better decisions and we certainly may be more motivated, when we are driven not just by our own need but the need of a loved one. My American Brother was no different, he had been alone for a few years and felt settled in England and instinctively knew this is where he would stay. The next step was to find a partner, this is where we see God answer prayer. My American Brother was lonely and wanted to discuss my views of Christian dating sites. I have no opinion really, I told him, however it is no different to CB radio which is how I met both my husbands, but that is for another day.

My American Brother was now braving the dating world, which is never easy when you have had a settled relationship and find yourself single again. The rules are always changing and naturally, as we get older, we carry the weight of our past with us. Of course, we know as Christians that the last thing God wants us to do is hold on to our past mistakes. If we seek forgiveness and work hard at following scripture and our Fathers' commandments, we are totally, wholeheartedly forgiven.

It is no surprise that negative experiences hit hard our self-esteem. No matter how deep our faith we are only human and while we strive to be more and more Christ-like, we continue to get knock backs. These shape our progress and make us better people, but they do not erase our fears and struggles. The loss of a relationship, a marriage, a long friendship can leave you stripped bare, vulnerable, and alone in the dark. My American Brother was no different, his previous relationship breakdown was based upon a medical condition that is never going to leave him. This stripped him of all confidence, after all this is something he could not change.

Understandably, it was with trepidation that he left early one morning to meet a Christian lady with whom he had been speaking with for some time. I waited for my phone to ring but not desperately waiting as I knew he was safe. I just wanted to know it had gone well or if the spark had been left on the park bench. I received a text saying he was home and as it was late, I left it till the morning to ask about his date. Overall, he had enjoyed the day, he described the lady as rather lovely and charming. Sadly, though she had telephoned after he got home to say she felt the medical condition was too much and did not feel she could take things any further. My American Brother was genuinely heart broken, after all what does that mean, how he was supposed to respond? I remember voicing my views on love not seeing disability. True love can overcome anything and although I agreed that long walks in the country were out of the question. If long walks is the thing you enjoy but un-accessible to the love of your life, then I felt that is what friends are for, to share the things your partner does may not enjoy.

I listened to My American Brother's story as we sat on his bed, we were family now. The lodger had disappeared months ago he was now my other brother. I ranted and paced about in the small area by the bed, where a rug would go if you had one. I could see this lady's perspective, but this was My American Brother and if you knew the love he had to give, the commitment not just to Jesus but to the people he cared about, you would compromise the world to hold onto that.

It turns out God had a plan, of course He had a plan! We had all prayed hard and asked for things to be blocked or allowed and our Father wants us to be happy for if we are happy, we can serve Him better. My American Brother needed this lovely lady and she needed him and with such a balance My American Brother would be able to carry on serving God. 'If it's God's will, this beautiful lady will call again,' said My American Brother and it was God's will! When She telephoned, she explained how prayer had led her straight back to him and could they meet again? So, they met again and again and one day soon after I got to meet this lovely lady. My American Brother was taking tea and eating many chocolate biscuits in my prayer garden. It is a small garden, perhaps six steps from back door to the summer house, which is where they were both sitting and holding hands. I am not sure if I wanted to meet this lady who at the beginning had such doubts, but she was lovely, beautiful and charming. While we chatted God's word, marriage floated into air and before I knew what was happening my dear American Brother had proposed to this beautiful lady!

My American Brother left us to move closer to this lovely lady and they would marry soon. It is so strange when you clearly see God's work. None of this would have happened if My American Brother had not moved in. He stayed almost a year and in that time his life changed completely. Our God is so good to us.

It is important to remember here that the more I see people in our church and beyond, obeying God, the more I see prayers being answered. The thing is accepting that we must obey God's word and commit our faith to Him before we are going to see any results. Even then the rewards may not be what we are looking for, but God knows what is best for us and how to get as exactly where he needs us to be.

Keep in mind PUSH: Pray Until Something Happens; be bold in your prayer and be prepared.

John 15:7

"But if you remain in me and my words remain in you, you may ask for anything you want, and it will be granted!"

I really connect with this verse when I think of My American Brother's situation. He has a true connection with Christ, a 'born again' believer and we are told when we are truly connected to the Vine we will bear the fruits that God has promised.

Who are your brothers and sisters of God?
Journal here!

†

24
ELIZA

My dearest friend had experienced the worst week ever with her daughter Eliza; hell had frozen over as the air in the family home turned blue with the foulest of languages. In fact, I stated at the time to Eliza, 'If you were able to place as much effort into foreign languages in lesson as you do with your swearing, you would be fluent by now!' I could empathise, after all I had been taught well by Alan. His rages were unthought out tribal communication, in a language I did not know.

Over time, experience taught me what was predictable and what responses were best from me. As I listened to my dear friend my empathy spilled over, the next sentence from my mouth was an offer of some space. Eliza arrived after school, her bags had already been dropped off, which allowed the family to have some much needed space - and where better to spend some time than in this tall skinny house that had offered some sense of well-being to all of its unexpected guests.

There was Eliza, camping out in the living room, as we had another guest in the spare room. For me it was simple, while you are here help with something, we all live and eat here, so do something for your keep.

'I will walk the dogs.' Eliza quickly offered.

The words were factual, no emotion, just fact. The tone said there was nothing else to add and nothing else Eliza was prepared to do, apart from gaming. This was okay, you cannot reboot and relax if another adult continues the debate, the problem just moves with you. I needed to be the break in the pattern of behaviour, so we chilled, and Eliza dog walked, ate and gamed.

Eliza is a name you sing, just as you would when you listen to Hamilton the Musical and Eliza comes in and has her own song. My daughter enjoyed this musical on repeat over the summer when Eliza came to stay, so it took no time at all for both of us to get into the rhythm of singing Eliza's presence in the room. I am unsure what Eliza actually thought of this but she would smile a tight-lipped smile, the type that is actuality hiding a full beamer but you really do not want anyone to know that life is good and that sometimes there are actually some funny bits in it too.

We had managed to get into a daily routine and the sofa worked well with its chunky large cushions being spread across the floor as a makeshift mattress; Eliza would get up and with help we would manage to get the living back to some normality. Although while she stayed, we never used the living room, allowing Eliza to have privacy and time to reflect in a quiet safe place.

'Eliza' Gertie-Grace sang and handed her a rather generous piece of cake. Twirling as she did so. Of course, the way too many teens' hearts is through their stomachs. Food plays a huge part in the life of some teenagers and it plays a large part in the life of the Salvation Army church. Mealtimes are a time to meet the most basic need of every human. If you have a full belly, and have had a drink, feel warm and have clothes, you are often more able to hear conversations, be open to support, access counselling and hear the Lord. The act of meeting the most basic need is the foundation on which trust is built.

Eliza enjoyed her food, her pupils dilated at the cake on the plate and off she went to consume her fill. She came back not half minute later, 'Is there any more Cake?' Wow! Now that really did go down a bit quickly, then Eliza explained.

'I put my plate down and as I did Penny jumped up and the cake was quickly gone.'

'Mm' I replied 'Yes, Penny will do that.' Penny is one of our Cocker Spaniels and she is a great believer that all food should go through her, and it does. I have never known a dog to consume so many scraps. Food is important to Penny and I am asking myself why she is not the Salvation Army mascot, as she holds the same values as the Church, meet my basic need and then we can start with anything else.

Dog walks were the only activity Eliza took part in willingly, as she enjoyed the company of our three cocker spaniels over the company of humans. Eliza had an online gaming presence and it was this virtual happy place that filled her otherwise dark empty void. I desperately wanted to remind Eliza that Jesus has far more worldwide presence than anyone; with the Bible still being the number one best seller. Why did I not say that go on and reinforce this message? Simply because all things are in God's time. My house at that moment was God's timing and Eliza was on her journey.

Eliza's mother had kept in touch while she stayed, we had prayed and hoped that we would all feel guided as to what steps needed to be taken to resolve the challenges that triggered so many arguments.

My Lieutenant spoke about a sermon he had heard; the story has an origin, but I cannot remember from where. A man was robbed, I believe he was a Vicar, he was thankful it was he that the mugger chose to rob. The thief took his wallet and the man was thankful that he did not have much money, so therefore he did not have much to lose. The thief had also left him with injuries, but he was thankful he was alive and that it was not someone else who was hurt.

We need to be more thankful; we need to break down our thanks to the little things, because they all come from God. We also need to remember that God is our loving Father, He does not want to see any of us hurt and broken. He knows life is tough, a challenge for each of us no matter our circumstances. He walks our journeys with us and when the light turns to dark and we sit in a pool of despair He takes our pain and turns it into something beautiful.

The beauty for Eliza's situation was to come in the decision to go and live with her father. It was a moment that numbed our hearts, to watch her make plans and pack all that she needed to travel half-way across England. We struggled, her mother and I, to see the Lord's reasoning in this - then it came to us. One night some months later, when Eliza called from her fathers phone to ask for money - Dad was drunk and they had no food. In fact, it was complicated, Dad was ill from abusing alcohol for many years and perhaps, for this short while, Eliza being present with her father was giving them time together, which there may not be in the near future. Her visit was one I will cherish, as we were privileged to be a part of her journey.

Romans 11:36

'For everything comes from him and exists by his power and is intended for his glory. All glory to him forever! Amen.'

Which simply means we owe everything to God. I read in a scripture Blog about how Paul's message is a reminder that all we do each day, is because of God. Waking up in morning, the good morning to a stranger, the route you took to work are all because of God's grace and mercy.

Psalm 139 tells us that "He knit us together in our mother's womb" I love this, the understanding that we all were thought about before the beginning of everything, each one of us so wanted and uniquely created. It is only by God's love and His mercy that we are here today, so all that we do needs to be for His glory. I find when I hold onto that I am the better person, when I keep this message alive, I live in the moment and I worry less, because I only need to do everything for the Lord, when He is my focus the details fall into place. What is so hard with that message is, my human nature needs to control, needs to know, wants to interfere; when I allow that instinct to be stronger than my faith, I usually find my world falls apart.

Notes.
Journal here!

25
TUROPHILE

The official word for someone who loves cheese is a turophile; the origin story for turophile can be traced to the Greek word for cheese, tyros, and the English ending -phile, for lover. (Thank you Google).

Turophile had literally only come to visit because of cake, which is ironic at the time as she was such a cheese lover. Turophile was a school friend of Jonathon's from the beginning of secondary school, she was not someone of whom Jonathon spoke much, so we had no real picture of her, until the cake invitation. Jonathon expressed his worry about his friend, who was turning tables in the classrooms and waiting for an autism assessment. When the result came through, she texted Jonathon saying I am autistic, and Jonathon texted back saying join the club, we have cake. Being autistic Turophile wanted to know where the cake was, who supplies it and when will she get her slice! Oh dear, I felt rather sad thinking about Turophile never getting her cake to confirm her membership to the most prestigious international club. So, I invited her over to have cake; this started my introduction to the minefield world that is gluten free. To be honest we seem better at it now, but ten years ago it was a real struggle to buy gluten free and making gluten free cakes was not an easy thing to do as I found the flour just would not bind with the rest of the ingredients.

Turophile became a frequent visitor, often coinciding with events linked to the Army Cadets. I noticed within weeks that Turophile had some real personal struggles going on and I felt that given time with the right approach I may be able to help her with these...but going back to the AC, she did this well. The structure suited her ASD and this enabled her to flourish as it allowed other hidden areas of her personality to come to the surface. But still she raged through my hallways when she visited. Her rages changed depending on the lack of understanding over whichever social situation she had hidden from. Life ticked by and Senior Prom came and went. This was a funny time as here was my Jonathon and Turophile, both preparing for the prom, both with blinkered thinking and approaches, fixed on rails that do not bend. Yet through scripting and a lot of planning they managed the Prom. At this point they were not an item just friends going to the Prom.

I am unsure at which point it became a thing, one minute it was just tomboy Turophile in the house and the next I noticed they were holding hands as they sat on the settle in the kitchen. It was just like that, we are going out now, so now we hold hands. The hand holding novelty lasted sometime and it is always reassuring to see your children form friendships rather than rush things just to get a relationship status on social media. I am sure it was between hand holding and actual dating, as in going out, that Turophile was at the house a lot more, far more than she was at home. It was at this time that I noticed the distinct lack of cheese in my house! Yes, hence the name, there is a great need to add a laughing emoji here. I would watch the gluten free veggie meals, yes also a vegetarian, come out of the oven and Turophile grate half a pound of cheese on top of it! I could not fathom what her problem was, well you could, eating to hide an awful lot of trauma. But oh boy that amount of cheese surely cannot be good for you.

Life continued and then Alan happened, so as the rest of world carried on, we became stagnant, decaying in our own shells, broken flesh, broken hearts, hope had left and the day to day treadmill seemed to hold no purpose. At this point Jonathon was in deep despair, we all were, but for the autistic mind, processing such a huge loss creates its own damage along with the trauma that has already set in. Jonathon decided to break up with Turophile, which he did with Emma in tow, she was standing just down the road to be the encouraging family member she was. The moment was not easy, Turophile wept loudly at the door and her mother screamed extremely loudly. Yet however much I think about that moment, the huge amount of hurt felt by both, I know it also made the relationship, it was the turning point.

Jonathon could not have imagined life without Turophile all the time Turophile was in it. He is autistic, he needed to play out the script to have some understanding of the moment he found himself in. The same applied to Turophile, all the hurt and all the tears allowed her to live an experience, to gain a measure of what she could cope with and where her wall was. God is so good, He is all seeing and His purpose, although not to cause hurt, made it into something useable. He equips as to help the next person, or to be prepared for the next event. In the case of Turophile and Jonathon, they met back up a few months later, all because I accidently telephoned Turophile on my contacts instead of Tiffany. I do not know a Tiffany but that's how close the names sat on my phone, so a rookie mistake. There I was asking Turophile how she was and she was not in a good place. I knew also that Jonathon had reached a critical low, so maybe now was a good a time as any to get these two together to see if there was anything left between them.

It turned out there was, Jonathon took Turophile to the same place they had their first date. They spoke a lot and then came home and there they both were sitting on the settle holding hands, we are back together now they informed me, "I see that" I said.

That moment led to Turophile experiencing great difficulties at home and of course her parents were concerned. Their daughter had been hurt and who knows what she might come up against. I mean, I would not like my son very much if the boot was on the other foot. But the boot belonged to my son and he was a bad person for a little while, according to Turophile's parents. We were in a mad moment ourselves one mealtime, with Turophile banging on our front door having pretty much run the half mile to our house, which for our cheese loving friend was a real effort. She was distraught, rasping for breath and enough tears were spilling from her eyes that could fill a teacup.

Which is a lot for this autistic teen who struggled to name emotions correctly, let alone feeling them in any usual driven way. There had been a fight at home, between the whole family, which had resulted in Turophile being the fallout zone, so she had left and brought her tears and frustrations to our Jonathon. Jonathon cannot do emotion, he fails to understand the context of what is going on; however, he will offer tea, because people seem to offer tea at a time of crisis. From across the kitchen we listened to Turophile tell a cascade of stories which were totally relatable.

The usual unfortunate misunderstandings of every autistic person, missing the cues to be quiet, not able to tell the pauses in conversations and so filling in the spaces and being told you are interrupting or worse that you are just rude. Then on top of that we struggle to see the usual perspective. We are great at thinking outside the box and coming from a starting point that is so off grid that nobody starts from there! My heart was broken for Turophile, she was stuck at an impasse and needed a way out, she also needed scripting to enable her to move forward in her life and grow emotionally.

As I wondered how to support her, she started raising her voice, her mum had texted to moan about Turophile's bearded dragons. It was then that I said, 'Well move the dragons here if it will help.' We had not had dragons yet. Rescued cats and the progression to dogs was going well and maybe the dragons moving in first, like a scout party was best. Turophile would need a lot of time and a lot of effort and I needed to put more thought to her situation before saying something I might regret.

The next day Jonathon asked Dad if he would go and collect Turophile's dragons, this was fine and Jonathon appeared pleased to be able to offer this help to his girlfriend. I stood at the door to watch the vivarium's come into the house, one then two and then some rucksacks and some bags and hey, Turophile had moved in with her dragons! The move your dragons here statement that I had casually made, of course meant you move in also, as unbeknown to me, where the dragons go Turophile goes also.

Turophile was not a well young lady, proportionally overweight, gut issues, huge anxieties, extreme low self-esteem, depression and a high number of tried medication. I decided to chat with her about Autism, how it appeared to me to impact on her and then I spoke about attachment disorder and trauma and how these things play a huge part in our responses to situations, our health and that there sits a fine line between Attachment or Developmental Trauma and Autism. Over time between family meetings and the building of positive scripts, we started to see change. The blurred picture that was Turophile was now becoming clear, as was her pretty face. The dark eye makeup had slowly changed and we could see the natural fresh face that sat beneath it. Sadly, we were still struggling with her weight, until one evening Turophile was in extreme pain and doubled over in the kitchen waiting for Jonathon to sort out a hot bottle.

"I don't need a pooh." she stated firmly before I could even open my mouth; okay boundaries were also still a problem! I sorted through the medication cabinet and carefully broached the subject of too much cheese. I followed this up with short articles and information on IBS. What we have learned with Turophile was that when she had an idea, she went full steam ahead in implementing it. This could have a catastrophic impact as she would address emotional issues immediately and overstep the mark causing a complete breakdown of relationships. An example of this was when Turophile forgot her key for the first time while living with us. In her world she reaches the house, rummages through her ruck sack, finds her key, opens the door to come in and then begins her home time routine.

"I have no key! OMG!"

Imagine the panic, the fear, it is equal to losing your phone.

The problem with many autistic people is the need for routine, it is this routine that gives some certainty to the day, which is very much needed in a world of so much uncertainty. Plus of course if you believe you have lost your phone, you leap into panic mode and hunt it down. No different to Turophile, blind panic had been activated.

This was all unbeknown to me as when I arrived home from work, everyone was in. I asked how their days had been and Turophile informed that me she had lost her key. I showed my concern then asked how long she had had to wait for someone; I knew that Gertie-Grace usually got home twenty minutes after Turophile. It was then I froze, as I saw the autistic panic unfold before me as Turophile informed me, she saw a stranger with a ladder and asked him to break in round the back! What? It is not easy to break into our home, as the only accessible way in is through the cat pen, a chicken wired covered basement that is the outdoor pen for my indoor cats. NOOOO! I felt sick bile in my throat as I listened about these two men who came through my house, passed my handbag, our friendly spaniels, our things in general on display. But that is what she had decided in her moment of her world breaking down, the need to follow that routine was greater than any sensible thought process. The fact of the matter is that when your routine unexpectedly changes, your world goes beyond red alert and reaches total wipe out; you cannot process it, it really is as if there is no room. Yet somehow, instead of the mind pausing and allowing time for the words to sink in. it won't. Something is squishing the information in, when there is no room. It physically hurts your head; I have been known to drop to the floor, complete shutdown or suddenly I am explosive, streaming out nonsense and anger – as if the yelling and spilling of words will somehow allow space for this new unexpected moment to be processed. My adorable niece explained it so well, our mind speeds with so much information, like Bo Burnhams internet song on repeat and loud! The thoughts running can seem so loud. Which is why the small child is unable to follow the instructions to go get their socks, or shoes, or sit still – all that is happening is the painful process of something else being squished in. There are others like this, some I have wiped from memory because the pain is too much. On our first Boxing Day together, a stranger came to my door and asked for Turophile. She came down and took a roughly wrapped parcel from him and he left.

Drugs I questioned to myself?

'What's going on?' I asked.

Oh, he was on face book offering out his left-over cheese! Who does this? Rather than go to him she gave out my address to a random person, because the thought of cheese going to waste was greater than any other decision she could make.

While not wanting to sound like a Wallace and Gromit film, I still had to voice that there was a need to have a conversation about cheese. Turophile needed to deal with the toxic areas of her life. We started with small conversations about why we behave as we do, our default trauma responses and of course, understanding autism. These conversations had a huge positive effect. In week one Turophile lost four pounds; I mean you could see it in her jaw line. In that first week I also still had cheese left in my fridge from last week's shop. The change continued and Turophile went from a size 18 to a size 16 then 14 and finally rested at 12. Wow I mean just wow, there she was just a young thing ready to take on the world. Actually, that is not true, the world is a big place for us with autism but certainly Turophile was stepping out of the front door with far more confidence than before. She had braved a visit to church, then following an Alpha course, had found God. She went on to find a rewarding job and discovered that life held so much more meaning. We had all grown in our relationships together and Jonathon and Turophile spent a lot of time laughing, it was such a huge change to witness over just three years. Then this year to mark the importance of family and to honour Alan's memory, Cherrie took her siblings, Turophile and our dear friend Jules to Disney Land Paris and there, just as the Disney park bus was unloading passengers from the fire work display, Jonathon proposed.

Through Turophile's tears, the little chest camera recorded in total darkness the voices of the masses saying things like: 'Sorry, oh excuse me, sorry, can I just squeeze by?' totally relatable and keeping life real.

We continue to move forward with Turophile and I have been privileged to see Jonathon and Turophile's relationship take on real depth. With autism you do wonder if it is possible to maintain relationships and think about the other people on whom you may have an impact. Turophile is a testimony that with scripting, support, and time, behaviour change can take place and emotional understanding can develop. The trick is to keep it going. If you leave the scripting alone and fail to build on it, then the work becomes undone. The understanding

Turophile has gained and the lessons she has built on are not a natural occurrence, she needs to remember her scripting each time she has a conversation. This is how I respond to questions, emotions, worry, confusion. This is what I do when I am unsure, lost, or in a panic. The scripts are endless and continuously being built upon. Life is full of so many variables that a new script is needed each day for the unexpected moments as the previous scripts will not fit the unexpectedness of tomorrow. The reassurance comes when you see such change in two people who without that effort and work, may not have managed to get us far as they have. If the dragons had not been invited in, we may not have got there at all.

> Hebrews 5:12-14
>
> You have been believers so long now that you ought to be teaching others. Instead, you need someone to teach you again the basic things about God's word. You are like babies who need milk and cannot eat solid food. For someone who lives on milk is still an infant and doesn't know how to do what is right. Solid food is for those who are mature, who through training have the skill to recognize the difference between right and wrong.

I have placed Hebrews here as I feel it reflects Turophile and Jonathon's journey; they both have needed teaching from scratch, learning social stories to manage each new social situation they have come up against. Each new day will often bring the need for a new script. This has given them both wisdom to ask and patience to plan their steps as they continue to practice their social stories, they both grow together and mature in their decisions.

Praise the Lord.

Do you know anybody like this?
Journal here!

26
ANNIKA

Galatians 3:28

There is neither Jew nor Gentile, neither slave nor free, nor is there male and female, for you are all one in Christ Jesus.

This verse reminds me why we took Annika in, Paul was speaking to the Galatians and his message was clear, we are all one in Christ, no matter our race or culture there is no value between us in our Fathers eyes. When I practice The Word, I find I can make clearer decisions as to what the right thing is to do. Trusting in the Lord and asking more and more about what he would do, helps us to be a part of something so much greater than anything we have on this earth.

I met Adrik before I met Annika, a tall well-built man in his late thirties, with dark tired eyes that have felt pain and a dark 5 o'clock shadow. I say tall, it is subjective, I am 5ft 2 and a bit, I think I stopped growing at 5ft 3 and now I am clearly shrinking. So many people are taller than me. Adrik was carrying with him a hammer and spoke English with a thick coating of a Russian accent. He said 'hello' and I was told by Carl, our lieutenant that Adrik was homeless and had come into our winter shelter with Annika. Annika has beautiful eyes. When I first met Annika she was frightened, relying on Adrik to translate for her and speak on her behalf (she is also deaf). I had little to do with Adrik and Annika for the first six weeks, I saw them both around the church and would say, 'Hi,' and smile. I made every effort to speak to Annika and to use google translate in short conversations. It was in March when I arrived at church, after the community breakfast, to see Annika clearly upset. Carl asked if I would sit with her and through expressive Russian and heartbroken tears, plus the use of google translate; Anika told me that Adrik is going to be deported.

For a painstaking month Carl gathered evidence for Adrik to stay, Annika in this time received an appointment for minor heart surgery and her GP requested also that Adrik stay. Adrik was a good man, however with the need for food on cold nights when you are homeless, often leaves you with two choices, no crime and stay hungry or feed yourself by committing a crime. Adrik had committed a crime, and so he was always going to be deported, no matter how many letters of support.

My Nick offered to drive Annika up to see Adrik at the deportation center, this was to be the last time she would see him and the trauma was clearly visible. She was heartbroken and cried out in pain throughout the days that followed.

When the time came for Annika's surgery, the lieutenant and his wife decided that Annika should stay with them. She had been sofa surfing at mine, as it seemed callous and cold to leave her desolate and alone on the streets. However, My American Brother was staying with us and we had no room, so the sofa had to do. Each night Annika would spread all the sofa cushions onto the small space on the floor and make her bed and each morning (I get up at 5am) the room would be back to living room standard. There was no way any of us would allow Annika to recover from surgery on my floor, and so she stayed short term with the lieutenant and his wife, two very patient people totally led by God.

The words 'Short Term' are never really that, I see them used a lot as a form of measurement, especially with temporary accommodation, it is only short term. What defines short term I am unsure. For Annika, she was meant to stay until she recovered, instead she stayed through the relocation of the lieutenant and his wife to another home and it was only at that point that pressure was placed for Annika to sort out something more permanent.

As Annika recovered, we managed to sort out her right to remain and claim universal credit. This meant that she was now in position to find a place to live. It was at this point that we learnt that Adrik had managed to get to Ireland and maybe we could get Annika to her husband after all.

Annika was so excited, Adrik had found work and had got a room in a hostel. We spoke about Ireland and how she might be able to continue learning English when she got there. Annika heart was light, she smiled a lot during this time. Then it happened, Adrik had been arrested, again. There was wailing, a lot of wailing. I think I would do the same if I realised that unless I give up my right to living in the UK, I will never see my husband again. I cannot imagine a life without Nick; it has taken thirty years and a lot of honest conversation to be the friends we are. I clearly see the gift God has given me in Nick. For Annika all cards were now off the table. To visit Adrik she needed money for the journey, money for a place to stay and money to buy food. The benefit system does not provide enough money, there is barely enough to live on. The time had come to grieve for the dream that was now lost and recognise the trauma that such a truth holds.

Do you remember My American Brother's love story in a previous chapter? He was getting married just at the time that Annika needed a place to stay, so of course we were able to offer her a place to stay, a chance to get sorted to make plans and move forward.

During December I prayed hard for Annika to have the money sent from Adrik to allow her to travel to Norway to stay with him. Sadly, this prayer was not answered. What happened instead was Annika's first experience of Christmas in England. She had bought beautiful gifts, wrapped so carefully and with great thought. These were handed out to the friends she made at college where she was learning English and to her Job Coach at the Job Centre. On Christmas day there were gifts for my family from Annika and we were able to share the love and thoughts back with some RUGS! (Really Useful Gifts).

I am unsure how different Christmas is here from Latvia, I doubt really there is much in it. We sit as family and share a meal, we celebrate family and our achievements, we share gifts as a recognition of our love to each other and Christ's birth. Remembering the love of Christ is one of the best things we can do, whether you believe in God or not. The love of Jesus is the purest love of all, unconditional, sacrificial and He offers the richest form of Grace and Mercy. When you look at that love and think about it, it is beyond comprehension. I become overwhelmed and need to fall to my knees with praise and thanksgiving, after all Jesus died the most horrific death to deliver me and you from our sins.

In a world where nothing is free, the one thing you have by simply asking God in prayer, is the forgiveness of sin and the strength to move forward in Christ each day. Following His teachings, growing in faith - it is all completely free.

Annika has this free gift; I did not know how deep her faith was until I bought her a Russian Bible. It was then as she took the book and beamed that I could see she loved the Lord our God. I knew she loved the Salvation Army, as she had sent me text after text thanking me for my time, telling me with many heart emojis that she loves the Salvation Army. I thought when I read those messages, that she meant it was because of the support she had received, but I understand now that she meant she loves God. The bible was a thank you for all her hard work, she does at the Salvation Army and I can say with hand on heart that nothing would be achieved at our Corps if we did not have our volunteers. Annika will work on the upper floor of our Hall, sorting through donations and bagging up recycling. She will work without a break for five hours, with continuous lifting and packing; sometimes I will need to direct her tasks to something more specific and without hesitation Annika will move onto something new. I see this as an act of faith. There is no question to my madness, just faith that I know what is needed to improve the service we offer, and Annika gets on and does it. I need to look more at this example when God shows me a different path and I question it, preferring the comfort of the old over the fear of the new.

Annika still lives with me. It has been eighteen months since she saw her husband and although she misses him dreadfully, she has built a life for herself. Annika is now studying English and has passed her first exam. I am pleased to say that there are continuous telephone calls between Annika and Adrik, their language is passionate and often loud, I am sure it is more frustration over the miles between them than an actual argument. What is so beautiful is that Annika loves being in England, she has made friends and has embraced all that is English. This passionate woman has experienced loss and trauma yet shows a strong loyal faith and a trust in God that we can all learn from.

Psalm 119:19

"Just as I feel excitement and wonder in travelling in a foreign land, so should I enjoy life everyday as I am just passing through."

How do you enjoy life everyday?
Journal here!

27
STEFANIE

I met Stefanie when I worked in health promotion with a children's fostering and residential service.

At the time my role was to ensure that she went to various health appointments and be the trusted person she could talk to. Being a trusted person does not mean that you will automatically get along with that person, there needs to be a common denominator. Fortunately, we both liked Dr. Who, we are both autistic, so quirky and awkward silences with misplaced conversations was not a problem. Again, being autistic does not mean you will automatically click with someone, however in this instance we did. I completely understood why it is was so difficult for Stefanie to wake in the morning. She had the trait of a busy mind and this meant no sleep until the early hours when, out of exhaustion, the mind finally gives in. I understood also that there were far too many other things to do than attend health appointments. In Stefanie's world her mind was so busy on the list of things she needed to achieve that she could never find a space within that list to get to a health appointment. I totally understood, but this did not change the task in hand. We needed to script in these valuable check-ups before all the professionals wiped her from their lists. The very moment we established some common ground we developed a trust which was to remain to this day. Appointments were set around lunch or supper. I have always found food to be a good reason for most teens to get out of bed or out of the house, away from any tech. Another good reason for Stefanie to come out to these appointments was the Dr. Who conversations we could have; I loved it! It meant I could go wild with my own theories that my own children had already dismissed as unpractical. Mostly they were dismissed as I did not have enough 'Old Who' memory and back story information, whereas with Stefanie, this was not an issue. We also had heaps of fun as store detectives, we would window shop before appointments or afterwards before food, calling into W.H Smiths or TK Max. Once in the shop we would separate and talk into our collars, as if speaking into a hidden microphone.

"Male, dark coat, 12 o'clock…KGB?" Yes, we were a little extreme and from that we developed our own spy game and laughed a lot. The only problem we had with this game was Stefanie's own keenness in ensuring I could hear her, so her voice would be a little louder than my own and most certainly in the ear shot of another customer. On many of these occasions, the blunt speaking, say what you see part of Stefanie would appear…

"Fat person, possible concealing weapons, to your left!" Not much wrong with that, we were playing, filling in those missed childhood gaps, but not so good if you were overheard. I would re-run my own scenarios as to what I would say if we were picked up by the real store security, fortunately this never did happen.

Now I need to be honest here, Stefanie has never actually lived here in our spare room but has probably spent the most hours here apart from Emma that is. This is because despite the government ruling that children may remain in foster care past their eighteenth birthday, it did not apply to children in a residential setting. To be honest, it does not really apply to children in care. Carers are no longer paid a fostering rate and the children must go on benefit and claim their rent. So often the dynamics change and it makes a mockery of the decision made that foster children should be allowed to remain with their carers. For if that is your only form of income, you then have to say I am sorry I am still unable to keep you here. When Stefanie turned eighteen it was time to leave the care system, at this time it was clear that she was not ready, and we did make an offer of the use of our room at that point, but the social worker refused that offer. They explained Stefanie would benefit from a supportive secure network that we already had in place and by her moving in with us, she may lose that.

It will not be a surprise to learn that I reached out to Stefanie and offered my home and family as a safe place to come. You know, if you are lonely, if you are stuck for food and of course if I felt I needed to check in on Stefanie, I would text; Fish n Chips and Dr.Who? This solved two problems, firstly it meant I could check up on her and explore how life was for her. Secondly it was an opportunity for Stefanie to get to know my family. What had not occurred to me was that Stefanie might be afraid of cats. At this time, we had six cats at home, five moggies and our pedigree Maine Coon, Zachary Binx, named after a character in Hocus Pocus. When Stefanie first visited it was painful to get her through her door, as she would walk almost with her back to the wall, fearful of every cat jump - I mean fearful. Her eyes would look everywhere and then she would ask.

'Is that one there?' 'No,' 'Is that one there?' She would literally flinch as she walked through our house, and then she would sit with her back to the wall so she could see any cats approaching.

Of course, with so many cats, there was always a cat there, none more than Binx. My silver haired beautiful proud Binx had spied Stefanie like a piece of prey...or so I thought. However, by week three, it was clear that he was not pestering Stefanie to fill her with fear, but more to ease her anxieties and show how beautiful and proud and calming the cat race is. This was the start a beautiful relationship. With time Stefanie would sit on the sofa with Binx sitting proudly on the arm of the sofa, always next to Stefanie. As the years passed Binx would make his way to Stefanie's lap and then when the kittens came, Stefanie had become a fully pledged cat lover. Or so I thought, but I had forgotten about Potter, who has his mother's eyes. I don't actually know if he does have his mother's eyes, it is just something we say in reference to his name, we also say; 'Potter what is this dark magic?' as he brings yet another dead bird to the front door. Potter is our half feral black tuft matted furred cat; he belongs to Jonathon simply because Potter chose Jonathon.

The problem we have with Potter is his sick sense of humour. He feels your fear and will swipe his right paw out and if you are not quick enough, you will be running for the tap and for kitchen roll. This 'swipe out' treatment is not just for the scared, no sooner do we fall for Potters sweet charm and distinctive purr he swipes! So, imagine the fun Potter was having with Stefanie. Oh, I forgot to mention the unusual charm that is Potter. He sits in wait for Jonathon to come home. When he sees Jonathon, he runs at speed and leaps in a pounce like motion onto Jonathon's shoulder, claws out to ensure a well gripped safe landing onto his shoulder. It really is a skill. After the first few years of Jonathon's shoulder being the runway for Potters' midair flights, we all soon became landing paths as well. I can tell you it really can be a shock if you are not expecting it. Out of nowhere your whole upper body jolts forward and this solid weight hits your shoulder, boom! Potter has landed.

Just as Stefanie had begun to build trust with the cat community in our home, thanks to Binx, Potter decided to take a run and leap on to Stefanie's shoulder...Boom! Once again, the fear of cats took over. Oh, my days there was such a commotion and along with it a healthy respect for our Potter.

Stefanie remains a huge part of our life, supporting the winter shelter at the Salvation Army, working in IT at a hotel, plus sharing all her IT gifts with the church community.

I do feel blessed to be 'Other Mother' to so many young people in my life. Coincidently when I visited a prayer garden on the outskirts of Kent, there was a kind lady who prayed with me and chatted about God's plan for me. She told me she saw that I was a spiritual mother and this was a gift from Jesus himself. Whether you have faith or are curious about what this life is all about, you must get a sense that there is a purpose hidden somewhere that you must know about. For me, as I greet yet another person to my home, I feel it, deep inside my soul that this person standing before me has been sent by Jesus to cross my path or my path to cross theirs, no matter which, it is clear that each is a part of a bigger plan.

How do you give back to the world?
Journal here!

28
TRIO

It never occurred to me that Trio would stay with us, at our home. Although none of our guests were ever expected, some had a buildup of conversation that left you with an inkling. For me this chapter lacks the flow of the being in the right place, but that awkward feeling actually mirrors the whole event. If we are honest we have all experienced those moments of complete awkwardness with guests or events in our life that become a part of our world, unconnected to anything and then leave, and we are left thinking... mmm I was not expecting that.

I met Trio when times were hard. He was homeless and part of the local council's Winter Shelter, which was run that year by the Salvation Army. Such a shame it can only do what it says in the title. Provide shelter for those on the street in the winter, as the funding from the local council is only enough for that critical time. Of course, the reality is that shelter is needed for more than just the colder months, a vulnerable homeless person is the same vulnerable homeless person whatever the season. Since Covid this form of temporary shelter has not existed, we wait to see if the new all year round provision remains funded post covid.

Trio needed as much support as the others in our shelter, what stood out was his willingness to please and help. He clearly, struggled with different areas of his learning but you could see there was no malice in him. Many who belong to the shelter become regular visitors to our church, mainly because we provide a community meal after the service.

What they do not expect to happen is that our Father has a way of ensuring they are held close and many keep on coming back and end up on our Alpha course. This is the greatest witness of them of all, not a bible reading, or speaking in tongues, or even a testimony, just the simple action of continuous kindness which shows God's love to everyone. At the time Trio became a part of the church so did Trinity, not out of homelessness but because she felt drawn to be connected to the church family. Trinity knew Trio from way back when and quickly became a supportive friend, a lovely girl with dark long hair and dark eyes. I thought, when I first chatted with Trinity, you could see she had a lot of autistic traits and I knew we would get on well. I loved her direct manner, which made me smile when she used a firm voice with Trio to curb his swearing. Of course, on some occasion's friendships lead to more and this what happened between Trinity and Trio.

First comes love then comes baby, which was a total surprise to Trinity who had been told that she could have no more children.

So here we are, two people whom God had bought together; two people who had children in care for varying reasons, two people who deserved a chance and now with the support to make this one work.

I heard once on Christian radio a minister asking how a couple in his church had managed to celebrate forty years of marriage. The main reason given was that you have got to want it. I thought this to be true, after all we all know how far we are prepared to go when we want something. God wants us so badly to see Him and to know Him that He sent His Son Jesus to be or Saviour and to die us.

The first thing you see when you see Trinity and Trio together, is that they want to be with each other. Trio wants to improve and be a better version of himself because he loves Trinity so much. Each person involved wanted the same outcome, for the support to be balanced and to promote independence, to ensure the home is was ready for baby. Plans were written up and agreed upon and just over fifty-eight hours later, Hope was born.

Courts are terrifying places to be, especially when they can change your life with one beat of your heart. Trio was there, unaccustomed to being in a suit, making every effort he needed, to keep his new family together. He had eaten at my house and chatted about the things he wanted to say, how scared he was and how he loved Trinity and hoped for so much. He did not want to see Trinity go through more pain of losing another child. So, I wrote it down in a text for him to read to the judge. I have never been so attached to two people in all my years of supporting families. My own loss and grief had resurfaced when I visited Trinity and watched her weep silent floods of tears as she cradled Hope for probably the last time and to have Trio on the phone, his voice breaking as he thought about the judge breaking his family apart.

I took my family dog walking, to distract myself from thinking about the case.

The nature reserve is stunning, its greens and yellows and browns blanket the marshes; God's tapestry to feed nature, providing a border to the sea beyond. My heart was flooded with emotion and I demanded from God that He act now. That is all I could do, a battle prayer, march around, demand and firmly ask my Father to provide His peace and His wisdom to all those involved in this matter.

As we trundled home my phone went, Gertie-Grace switched to hands free, it was Trinity, her throat was raw, as she had been crying.

Any news I asked stupidly, a tourniquet around my heart.

Her tears flowed and she told me she had got the mother and baby placement. Praise God.

I cried, Gertie cried, Trinity cried.

That evening as I settled into bed early, Nick was due to go on another midnight shift I was feeling exhausted and emotionally drained, when the door went. The dogs barked, leaping all over the sleeping Nick, and I rushed out to the front door. There was Trio, red eyed from crying, standing on my top step looking totally lost. He told me he just could not sleep, he felt overwhelmed and did not want to be in his own. I waved him in and showed him to the spare room. Once in there he fell onto the bed and slept like a baby.

At the point of writing Trio was my latest guest, there is no end to hospitality or indeed his family story. We wait, with plans in place to clean and organise the small studio flat, ready for Trinity and Hope to come home to. Prayers will be said continuously as it is by prayer and petition...

We will trust in God I told Trio, we cannot control the decisions of local authority, all we can do is be ready and trust in our Father to know what it is we need. What I know for certain is that God wants us to live everyone as Jesus does, to only reflect His love. Trio Trinity and Hope are easy to love and placed before us as part of God's plan, so we are committed for the long term, whatever happens.

The whole situation bought to mind this verse, which speaks about being saved by the lord and if you believe so will your household. Trinity has a simple faith for God, she is spiritual, and her belief needs no more than that God Loves her and she will be fine. This simple act of faith would impact on Trio and continue to support their journey, which turned into one of weekly visits and foster care. As the days moved and a year passed these visits remain in place, meaning that prayers were answered and the Trio have their sense of family.

Acts 16:31-34 - And they said, "Believe in the Lord Jesus, and you will be saved, you and your household." And they spoke the word of the Lord to him and to all who were in his house. And he took them the same hour of the night and washed their wounds; and he was baptized at once, he and all his family. Then he brought them up into his house and set food before them. And he rejoiced along with his entire household that he had believed in God.

How is your faith?
Journal here!

29
FORTEM

The word Fortem is Latin for Brave and its important you know that it was agreed upon by my house guest to use this name to represent them. To be honest they were not feeling brave and in fact felt that the whole journey of finding their way to my home was a bit like a neon signpost that read 'Failure' in hyper flashing yellow! At that time the failure was purely internal like a parasite eating its way down to your core. Through self-ridicule and self-sabotage, the failure became a solid object to carry. It was at this point that I first became fully aware of Fortem, sitting in my kitchen, dark glossy locks falling around a pale face and framing dark eyes. Almost Italian looking and carrying the genetic curves of all the best mythical goddesses. There they sat, upset, angry, and unable to express what exactly the problem was. I mean to say from my point of view, there is always two sides, but I am always frustrated when young people are mis-understood and when battles are fought unnecessarily. Of course, any battle for a teenager is unnecessary, and I only know this because of the many battles I had with my Alan, each a complete waste and each achieving nothing. Yet as parents we still drag them through no-man's land in the hope of proving some point or another. I was the world's worst at this, for a while. The process is soul destroying, it is often humiliating and often adds to the trauma; they stack up like Jenga bricks. What hindsight has given me is a knowledge of Adverse Childhood Experiences. I understand now that what was happening each time Alan and I fought, was simply both of us were re-triggering each other's trauma. In that moment, neither of us were able to make sense or communicate, only rage rocked the boat until the sea was calm again. Our arguments were fierce, though we loved each other. I fondly remember when Alan was twenty, being told by him that he thought I was cool now I had grown up and he was impressed with my knowledge.

So here we are, with a problem and only Fortem has the capability to spin an academic approach to family drama. Their stance on such complex matters is mature; there was always the possibility that they were at fault. Then the frustration that they could not make themselves understood and finally the child would come out and the expletives would begin. After the dictionary had been unpacked, the tobacco would follow and then there was calm.

The day Fortem temporarily moved in, was the day when we could no longer move past the expletives. It was also when the house was full, so the cushions came back off the sofa and the lounge back into a bedroom.

On the first night, Gertie-Grace and I sat talking in whispers, she was sure Fortem was going to freak out. The whole situation was too big as it was; arguments with parents and siblings are never easy and in Fortem's case always explosive. I was expecting that she would adjust to a change of routine with ease and simplicity, though I'm not sure why I thought this. I guess I figured that Fortem was used to sleeping at one friend's home or another, why would mine be any different? The phone vibrated and vibrated again. Fortem announced she was freaking out, she could not stay, she did not know where to go but she could not stay. Gertie-Grace had called it and now was on damage control, as she reassured, rearranged, and rescheduled the lives of everyone at home to ensure the quick settling of Fortem to the family routine. God is so good, we were hardly inconvenienced with Fortem's stay, there was not much to discuss, just the need for space, time to process events and plan the next steps going forward. Most of the next steps were discussed with chocolate cake or brownies as an aperitif to the conversation. I have a lot of time for cake, after giving up alcohol, to become a Salvationist and smoking many years before; cake became by measure of 'disaster darling'. At the end of a bad day, you need a custard tart, lemon tart, maybe a tougher day requires a pastry. So, I need no convincing that anything that measures larger than a tough day requires fresh cream in various settings, generally apple turn over, or chocolate cake. However most cream cakes will add calm, providing a thinking space as you stop to drink tea and take a bite.

It's never easy to know what is best, especially when it's our own child we have fallen out with. I am by nature a fixer and I find it impossible to leave things alone. I need to know that we are okay, that information has been understood. Fortem's family left things alone, and this taught me a great lesson for reflection, when considering areas of my family dynamics.

One of the first needs I recognised in Fortem was the need to connect with her young man. I am unsure if at this stage they were girlfriend and boyfriend, although from Fortem's point of view it was easy to see that the center of her world was this chap and so the kindest thing I could do was allow her to invite him in for a brew. Sometimes the simple act of setting your eyes on someone you care about is enough to ease the most heightened anxiety, providing chicken soup for the soul.

What became clear to me was that God's purpose for Fortem's brave voice; we forget that our Father is a teacher that through Him all things are made. We do not spare a thought that through the most challenging of times we can learn the most valuable lessons. We remember this with hindsight, but during the storm we are fearful, like Peter on the boat calling out to the Lord to be saved. I am sure, without any doubt that Jesus stands beside me as I struggle against the storm, willing me to see that He is there. Yet still I cry out in prayer asking our Lord Jesus to come. For Fortem, I believe her challenges are spiritual, although very earthly; the actual message we always came back to seemed to be centered around life choices and moral dilemmas. Whether it was to do with the 'here and now,' or how can life be so complicated and for many raised through church, what is it I believe in? Whatever it is, I am sure we are all in agreement that growing up is incredibly difficult. I do feel that there is more today for young people to contend with, and that if they have no access to a trusted person, the problems can magnify very quickly. My prayer is that within it all, each struggling young person finds their Fortem and talks to someone. What comes to mind is:

Deuteronomy 31:6

"Be courageous, don't tremble, don't be afraid, the Lord your God is with you, He will never leave you."

These words are not an offer of help you can refuse with a shrug; they are a statement of fact. The Lord your God is with you, He will NEVER leave you. Holding those words in your heart and believing it in your soul, will allow you to find your Fortem.

†

30
THE BEGINNING

I have been asked to chat about the first time I met my husband Nick; at the time I only knew him as Maverick; I was happily married to Keith, we had just had our second child Cherrie and she was just four weeks old. Keith worked for P&O ferries; this meant a week away from home every fortnight. It was a challenge not having him home, however the benefits were that when he was off, he achieved so much DIY in our home. The latest project was the MFI oak kitchen. It looked amazing, with an island work surface separating the kitchen and dining room, opening space in the once damp dark galley kitchen.

I had OCD traits in my younger years, placing my energy on housework, organising my days with the children, and running timetables along with menus for dinner. It was 7pm on a hot August evening and both children were resting. Cherrie was asleep but Alan never slept, he was listening to audio books. Bottles were made up for the night and I was sitting in the utility room chatting on CB radio to the few people I had met.

The CB radio I feel was equivalent to social media today and probably a lower risk, as people you chatted to were local. I had met Keith through Citizen Band Radio. My mother had sadly lost her sight at the age of 34; with the loss of her sight came the loss of her job. In the late seventies' disability was just that, you were now a worthless commodity reliant on government benefits. Fortunately for mum, she had been given a Blue Peter guide dog, Fergie. This opened opportunity to visit local schools and speak at local events. It also meant that she became known and the CB community wanted to open her world to further support from a generally trusted radio community. This meant that there was always someone to talk to however late it got. For mum, the white noise between breaks of the mic made her feel sick. Her anxieties grew at the thought of people knowing where she lived and so she never used the radio. It sat highly polished on the coffee table until I plucked up the courage to key the mic and say one nine for a copy...and so began my learning curve.

During Keith's and my time together, we had kept the CB radio. Keith liked the idea that I had access to people who can help me in a time of crisis. I was so naive that it had not occurred to me he was sleeping with most of the women he spoke to, I was too trusting and too in love to see anything but good in Keith. If we argued, I believed him - it was my fault. If the bills were too high, I believed him - I needed to make more effort. If he was out late or not home, I needed to put my insecurities away as that did not build relationships. Keith would hold my hand and stroke my thumb rhythmically and I willed myself to hold onto his words, after all I needed to think of the children. Alan was two years old and head banging on all manner of concrete surfaces, not sleeping, and showing signs of ADHD. Cherrie had just come into the world but had already adapted and managing to regulate her sleep pattern within the first month. We were fortunate to have Cherrie, she was a blessing from God, a much-wanted baby by me, so much so, that I had counted religiously my period days to work out my best days for ovulation. I remember a particular strong argument between Keith and myself. I was convinced he was sleeping with a colleague on the ferries. This conviction came from strong evidence I had recently recovered from a STI and knew that it was not me who had been 'sailing' into other harbours! After we argued Keith took the antibiotics, but things were strained between us. He went back to work but when I next ovulated, I contacted him to meet up to chat things through. After all I was head over heels; needless to say, one thing led to another and Cherrie was going to be called Cherry after the Bright Yellow Datsun she was conceived in.

Sadly, my timing was pants, Keith had not planned for another child and any happiness faded to the acceptance that both Keith and I were perhaps always going to struggle. We loved each other with a passion but could not find a balance where we could live together without the same passion turning to arguments. On each of these moments sits unresolved trauma, my own from my childhood and Keith's from his; this is no fault of our parents, just how it was then. We know better now, professionals have access to longer studies and now our own local council, as others have done, are aiming to be trauma informed across all areas by 2023.

The CB radio enabled me to feel less isolated as a mum who was running ragged after a small boy who at this point was undiagnosed autistic, ADHA and bipolar. I was able to chat to people about mundane things, meet the small local radio community and get involved with events. To be honest most events involved drama and gossip and often meant I was repairing and fixing other people's lives.

On the day I met Nick, we had already been chatting on the radio for about four months. Keith was on his weekly rote and I had the children settled. It was particularly hot and it had been a mild winter. Between Cherrie and Alan's daily routine I had been obsessively picking up rolled up dried jelly pieces of cat food of the kitchen floor. Mozart, our cat, was not usually a messy eater but over the last week this had become a regular event for me.

Despite it being about 8pm, it was still warm and bright, the stable door of the utility room was still open and as I sat listening to people chat, I heard Andy call out and announce his arrival. I had known Andy about a year, he was a sweet young man who had dated a beautiful young lady named Nicole, I think. As with young relationships, they broke up but we had remained friends and Andy always checked that I was safe when Keith was away. This was a blessing as it was Andy who would rush me to A&E six months later with a very ill Cherrie. For now, he was checking in and we sat drinking coffee and I leant down yet again to pick up some dried cat food. It was at this point that everything changed, firstly Andy commented on the rattle in the back of the new fridge. I explained it had been rattling all week and that Keith was going to look at it when he got home. I then told him about the dried-up cat food and he peered at the piece I had picked up in the kitchen roll.

"That's not cat food," Andy pointed out, "You've got mice!"

"Ewwwe!" I leapt up and reached for the Milton. As I rummaged around for cloths, Andy placed his hands either side of the top corners of the fridge and shifted it forward a notch...as he did so the familiar rattle changed tempo and the long brown gorged body of a well-fed rat raced across the kitchen floor in between the oak plinth of the utility room cupboard.

A quote from Four Weddings and a funeral fell from my mouth, I will alter it slightly to save the burn to your ears.

'Duck, Duck, Duckity, Duck!'

My heart raced as I thought about where the rat had scurried, how many days had it been since I was picking up rolled up pieces of cat food? I felt sickened, a complete ice cold washed over me, followed by tiny hairs rising on my arms and back of the neck. I thought about the children and a thousand scenarios raced through my head. None of them ended well, and many of them included spaniels and Siamese cats, ooops a Disney cross over, must be lack of sleep!

I looked at Andy; 'What shall we do?'

'Go hunting,' was his response...and he reached for the mic and keyed it:

'One nine for a copy'. Then he sang out UB40's song... 'There's a rat in my kitchen what am I gonna do?' It was the beginning of an exceptionally long night.

I picked the phone and rang the local station. It seems very strange that I did this, as now we would go through to a main switchboard, but on this day in 1990, our local office was taking calls.

'Do you know anyone with an air rifle?' asked the officer. I mouthed the words to Andy who said 'yes'... so I said 'yes' to the officer and the officer said,

"Well there is your answer." Andy once again pressed the mic;

'Nineteen Frog Pond, does Maverick have an air rifle? Jade's got a rat in the kitchen.' The giggles came back and this was the first response before any actual conversation that night.

I knew Maverick to talk to, in fact he was a complete flirt and good for a laugh and on this day completely drunk. Andy offered to pick Maverick up and bring him to Jade's twenty if he brought his air rifle. Maverick agreed, so Andy left.

I did what any girl would do with a new baby sleeping upstairs and a rat in her kitchen downstairs, I rang my mum.

My mum sent down my brother with Fergie her guide dog and not just any guide dog but the Blue Peter guide dog. I am unsure why Fergie came; my cat Mozart had been completely useless, so I held no hope out for the dog. My brother knocked at the door and came in. He looked apologetically at the dog lead in his hand and said he dare not ask for explanations.

As Bro arrived so did the rain, the weather was humid and a storm was needed, and here it was. The rain was falling hard and I saw headlights reflected on the glass in the front door, here was Andy and he was with Maverick.

I raced down hall and opened the door, Andy came in clutching an air rifle and behind him was a chap in jeans and t-shirt, and shoulder length curly hair. He had huge round glasses on and looked almost like John Lennon. I watched Maverick climb over the bonnet of Andy's car and walk up my garden path to stand in front of me and question... 'Why are all the best ones married?' Then he walked into the kitchen and he saw my brother un-doing the kitchen plinth to get the rat out.

'You weren't kidding then,' said Nick and threw down the pellet tin and opened it up to tell my bro to skin up while he loaded the rifle!

I am unsure where we are with the time at this point, there were conversations. I know I would have bottled fed Cherrie and my brother carried her around for bit, but that would have been that; she was an exceptionally good adaptable baby, from the word go. That is another chapter for another day. Cherrie is so meant to be, timed to the moment of conception and a gift from God, as we all are. Just read and reflect on psalm 139, it is all there.

We had settled into a pattern of teamwork; I oversaw refreshments and keeping the CB Radio community updated with events. The police had telephoned to ask if they could help any further, at this point Maverick, as in Nick and my brother were stoned, so I thanked the officer and told him it was all under control. Maverick, Bro and Andy had unscrewed half of the brand-new utility room when suddenly the rat ran out and dived through the smallest of gaps in the make-shift barricade that the men had put up to stop the rat running out of the utility room! My jaw dropped as I watched the elongated brown creature run across the kitchen floor, Nick grabbed the rifle and fired pellets at the rat only to see them land in the new Lino floor and the rat escape up the back of my brand-new cooker.

What now? The science of any man can be intriguing; I often find the male thought process makes no sense to me at the best of times. Young men, under any influence can become creative and foolhardy. I was still perched on the kitchen worktop and had literally given up on any outcome, especially as now my brother had decided that lighter fluid squirted down the connective metal brace at the back of the cooker, would cause the rat to fall out and then of course Nick could shoot it.

I cannot say to this day who thought that turning the oven on was a good idea, but it was now 4am, I was exhausted and the kitchen was a mass of teacups as well as various empty crisp packets, along with half eaten biscuits all opened during mini munchie episodes that Bro and Nick had endured during a late night of hunting.

I had gone to the loo and as I walked downstairs, I could smell burnt hair. It really was an awful smell and as I walked into the kitchen to put a stop to all the commotion, the rat rushed out from behind the cooker. It took only one shot for it die and skid across the kitchen floor. I felt sick, I felt relived, I felt like I wanted to cry. Prior to that day I had never hurt a living creature and since that day I have never hurt a living creature. I know needs must, but still it was just sickening. I know also that the winter the year before was too warm and so there were lots of rats, but it does not change the fact that the moment was awful, the moment stuck for a long time.

The rat had died, Nick looked up at me and asked when the fry up was and by 5am we were all eating. My lovely, wonderful mum was knocking on my front door, armed with cleaning bits and instructions for me to go to bed and she would sort Alan and Cherrie out.

The following evening Keith came home and listened to the story, he also had to put the kitchen back together again. He met Nick and they both went on to be good friends for a long time. In fact, Keith's mum Ivy came to our wedding and Keith sent a lovely card wishing us both the best.

'I know the plans I have for you' declares the Lord…and He does. It's one of the verses I draw upon the most because we don't see it, we forget to look and we are often unaware. We then panic and interfere with God's plan, which is always for the good. With hindsight I see them all, how my Father has placed me in situations to skill me up, build me up, rescue me, lead me, provide hope for me.

My alternative verse to Jerimiah is Isaiah 55:8-12

"My thoughts are nothing like your thoughts," says the Lord.
"And my ways are far beyond anything you could imagine.
For just as the heavens are higher than the earth,
so my ways are higher than your ways
and my thoughts higher than your thoughts.
"The rain and snow come down from the heavens
and stay on the ground to water the earth.
They cause the grain to grow,
producing seed for the farmer
and bread for the hungry.
It is the same with my word.
I send it out, and it always produces fruit.
It will accomplish all I want it to,
and it will prosper everywhere I send it.
You will live in joy and peace.
The mountains and hills will burst into song,
and the trees of the field will clap their hands!

When I reflected on this verse I think about how God's thoughts are boundless, and we occupy all of his thoughts. Sadly, the thoughts of men and women are fixed on the things they achieve and we measure an entitlement to our actions. We foolishly think that our own actions will save us, yet when we look at the Lord's thoughts, he freely forgives, his grace is endless, he is the only one that can save us. Both Jerimiah and Isaiah are about completely surrendering to God and then we will see and gain and so much more.

I am totally humbled by His presence, that Jesus should want to look after me, forgive me, to give His grace and mercy to me, when I am so unworthy. When I think of how I met Nick, how strange those circumstances tied in as they did. Even when I was single again, I still did not see myself with Nick, it was my mother who insisted I at least accept the offer of a date.

It was the worst date, not good. Involving a broken toe, - snow conditions and a desperate need to get back from Canterbury to my Mums and just sit and be with the kids. In hindsight this date and each subsequent half-baked successes we have enjoyed together, have all gone to build resilience into our relationship. Maybe, this is the reason we were able to cling onto our marriage after Alan; the Lord knows I tried so hard to push Nick away, we were all totally broken, nothing can be said to heal the pain, there were no words. Just a silence, a gulf, a void, and a need to crawl into a pit of nothingness. While the loss impacted on all of us, we were all on different carriages that is the journey of grief. We will reach the same destination, get to a place where you can carry the baggage. Yet the travelling, on occasion, would wipe you out. Alan had mental health issues and I am sure I have said it already, he was not going to make old bones. God ensured I had Nick, my Father blessed us and protected us, ensuring that while we travelled the journey of grief, we had Nick at the controls.

In 1 Kings 18: 41-46 We see Elijah send his servant seven times to look for rain, and after the 7th time the servant reports seeing a small cloud the size of your hand. I left Keith 7 times and went back six. It was the 7th time that I managed to stay away and heal the hurt I carried. This reminds us that God is good with promises, although the horizon of our life seems empty, just beyond it is the hope we are looking for, the answered prayer, the open door. It may not always be what we asked for; however, the answer will always come...so do not give up.

Elijah Prays for Rain.

Then Elijah said to Ahab, "Go get something to eat and drink, for I hear a mighty rainstorm coming!"

So Ahab went to eat and drink. But Elijah climbed to the top of Mount Carmel and bowed low to the ground and prayed with his face between his knees.

Then he said to his servant, "Go and look out toward the sea."

The servant went and looked, then returned to Elijah and said, "I didn't see anything."

Seven times Elijah told him to go and look. Finally the seventh time, his servant told him, "I saw a little cloud about the size of a man's hand rising from the sea."

Then Elijah shouted, "Hurry to Ahab and tell him, 'Climb into your chariot and go back home. If you don't hurry, the rain will stop you!'"

And soon the sky was black with clouds. A heavy wind brought a terrific rainstorm, and Ahab left quickly for Jezreel. Then the Lord gave special strength to Elijah. He tucked his cloak into his belt and ran ahead of Ahab's chariot all the way to the entrance of Jezreel.

31
TO CONCLUDE

These pages and the time taken to pen this book initially were slow, mainly because the whole exercise has been cathartic. Through the Rabbit Hole, I cried as I was re-triggered with trauma and re-living the journey. As I edited the Rabbit hole, I cried again for different reasons, the gratitude I have for the Lord's grace and His mercy, I am full of sin, we all are. Yet despite this Jesus opened His arms and gave Himself away for us.

Then Covid happened and I believed for a breath of a moment that I would have nothing to do. Instead, the need for our food bank placed high demand on the church as it did internationally. So, my time and my faith went on a new journey and already the new book with twenty other beautiful moments, is being penned in my head. Covid has a wealth of experiences attached to it, a million tears imprinted on it and a thousand positives that have come from it. I feel, that out of respect to the homeless community and the local residents who served through it, lived through it and cried through it - that these stories should be shared. Then there is God's prompting and the Lord gave us Bill and Bill gave the title of book two; as he wandered into church one wet morning at 5.50am and stated a fact, "I don't know what I would do if you weren't here Jack...I mean...where will I get my socks from? There it was, the next title; and the question raised by many homeless people through our door 'Where will I get my socks from?'

All who know me
who know my heart,
you know I thank
you for each players
part.

Isaiah 40:31
But those who hope in the Lord, will renew their strength, they will soar on wings like eagles; they will run and not grow weary, they will walk and not be faint.

Thank you for reading, Hope you enjoyed it.

1 Corinthians 16:14: Let all you do be done in LOVE

Thank you, God.
In Christ Alone
Jacqueline.

www.ingramcontent.com/pod-product-compliance
Lightning Source LLC
Chambersburg PA
CBHW071604080526
44588CB00010B/1019